Poltergeists

Poltergeists

New and future titles in the series include:

The Mystery Library

Poltergeists

Stuart A. Kallen

LUCENT BOOKS

An imprint of Thomson Gale, a part of The Thomson Corporation

Detroit • New York • San Francisco • San Diego • New Haven, Conn. • Waterville, Maine • London • Munich

THOMSON

GALE

© 2005 Thomson Gale, a part of The Thomson Corporation.

Thomson and Star Logo are trademarks and Gale and Lucent Books are registered trademarks used herein under license.

For more information, contact
Lucent Books
27500 Drake Rd.
Farmington Hills, MI 48331-3535
Or you can visit our Internet site at http://www.gale.com

LIBRARY OF CONGRESS CATALOGING-IN-PUBLICATION DATA

Kallen, Stuart A., 1955–
  Poltergeists / by Stuart A. Kallen.
    p. cm. — (Mystery library)
  Includes bibliographical references and index.
  Contents: Poltergeist phenomena—Poltergeists, possession, and exorcism—Hunting poltergeists—Poltergeist communications—When poltergeists attack.
    ISBN 1-59018-321-5 (hardcopy : alk. paper)
  1. Poltergeists—Juvenile literature. I. Title. II. Series: Mystery library (Lucent Books)
  BF1483.K35 2005
  133.1'42—dc22
                                                                    2004024599

Printed in the United States of America

Contents

Foreword

In Shakespeare's immortal play, *Hamlet*, the young Danish aristocrat Horatio has clearly been astonished and disconcerted by his encounter with a ghost-like apparition on the castle battlements. "There are more things in heaven and earth," his friend Hamlet assures him, "than are dreamt of in your philosophy."

Many people today would readily agree with Hamlet that the world and the vast universe surrounding it are teeming with wonders and oddities that remain largely outside the realm of present human knowledge or understanding. How did the universe begin? What caused the dinosaurs to become extinct? Was the lost continent of Atlantis a real place or merely legendary? Does a monstrous creature lurk beneath the surface of Scotland's Loch Ness? These are only a few of the intriguing questions that remain unanswered, despite the many great strides made by science in recent centuries.

Lucent Books' Mystery Library series is dedicated to exploring these and other perplexing, sometimes bizarre, and often disturbing or frightening wonders. Each volume in the series presents the best-known tales, incidents, and evidence surrounding the topic in question. Also included are the opinions and theories of scientists and other experts who have attempted to unravel and solve the ongoing mystery. And supplementing this information is a fulsome list of sources for further reading, providing the reader with the means to pursue the topic further.

The Mystery Library will satisfy every young reader's fascination for the unexplained. As one of history's greatest scientists, physicist Albert Einstein, put it:

> The most beautiful thing we can experience is the mysterious. It is the source of all true art and science. He to whom this emotion is a stranger, who can no longer wonder and stand rapt in awe, is as good as dead: his eyes are closed.

Noisy Spirits

Scientists have provided answers to many of the world's mysteries. They have cured diseases that have cursed humanity for millennia, manipulated human DNA, and sent spacecraft to circle the rings of Saturn. There are some mysteries, however, that have escaped scientific explanation. In the realm of the supernatural there are still few solid facts known about the sources of poltergeist activity.

While the causes of this supernatural phenomena are unknown, the effects of poltergeists have been well documented for hundreds of years. As long ago as the twelfth century, Reginald of Durham, an English monk also known as St. Goderic, was said to witness poltergeist phenomena. Stones rained down inside Reginald's humble apartment, furniture and other objects were hurled about by invisible forces, and a container of wine flew through the air and poured itself over his head. At the time, the common belief was that these disturbing events were caused by rambunctious ghosts or other demonic creatures who either acted alone or worked through possession of innocent victims. By the fourteenth century, these destructive, malicious ghosts in Germany were called rumplegeists—rumbling or jostling spirits. Because their alleged activities were often loud and disruptive, sixteenth-century religious reformer Martin Luther labeled the ghosts "Polter-Geister," or noisy spirits. Oddly, while the word is in widespread use in English-speaking countries, it is not used today in Germany, where a poltergeist is known as a "spuk," or spook.

Whatever they are called, poltergeists have been blamed for a wide range of bizarre pranks including breaking objects, provoking spontaneous fires and floods, whipping up strong winds on a calm day, and even placing excrement in food or on walls. Some have even said they were pinched, bitten, hit, or sexually assaulted by poltergeists. Such activities are known to start and stop abruptly, as opposed to more "normal" ghostly activity that can continue for decades or even centuries. Sometimes the activity lasts only for a few hours or days; other times it can continue off and on for several years.

PK Energy

Some paranormal researchers, or parapsychologists, have questioned the concept of poltergeists as ghosts. Instead they believe that poltergeist activities are a result of victims emitting intense mental energy that affects the physical environment.

Poltergeists sometimes demonstrate their presence by hurling household items. In this early twentieth-century illustration, kitchen utensils reel before a frightened cook.

This concept is referred to by the unwieldy name "recurrent spontaneous psychokinesis," or simply RSPK or PK energy. (The term *psychokinesis,* or "mind movement," is derived from the Greek words *psyche* or "mind" and *kinein* meaning "to move.") By using PK energy, people can allegedly bend spoons, make objects fly around the room, cause odd rapping noises in walls, create foul odors, and even manifest gooey slime, called ectoplasm, on walls, ceilings, and floors.

This kitchen has allegedly been disturbed by poltergeists. Some researchers believe that poltergeist activity is actually caused by people harnessing psychokinetic energy.

Like so much else surrounding poltergeists, however, there are doubts about the source. Not all researchers agree that PK energy is responsible—or that it even exists. As parapsychologists Alan Gauld and A.D. Cornell write in *Poltergeists:*

> We do not know sufficient [information] about psychokinesis . . . as investigated in certain sorts of laboratory experiments to say whether or not it has any kinship with poltergeist phenomena. And we must not slip into thinking that because we have applied to the phenomena a scientific-sounding rubric like "RSPK" we are somehow nearer to explaining them. At least it should be clear to everyone that labeling a certain obscure phenomena "poltergeist" phenomena no more explains them than would calling them "goblin" phenomena or "gremlins."[1]

With even the experts disagreeing, it is doubtful there will soon be an explanation for the frightening activities of poltergeists. Of course there are many who do not believe in poltergeists, ghosts, or any other paranormal activities, which they attribute to the overactive imaginations of the victims. Those who have studied poltergeists disagree. In the future a technological breakthrough may result in an invention that can prove once and for all if poltergeists really exist. For now, the answers lie beyond the reach of science.

Chapter 1

Poltergeist Phenomena

Stories of troublesome ghosts are common to every age and culture. Sometimes these spirits are said to appear in visible form, as fog, light, or ghostly images of the formerly living. However, one particular category of spirit, the poltergeist, almost always remains invisible. These entities make their presence known by creating commotion, throwing objects, making cacophonous noises, starting fires or floods, or emitting odd, sometimes repulsive, smells. For centuries, these bizarre events were blamed on confused ghosts who did not realize they were dead and tried to return to living bodies. By crashing about between this world and the afterlife, these apparitions purportedly generate chaos, as Herbert Thurston writes in *Ghosts and Poltergeists:* "[Poltergeists] enter houses and turn everything upside down, doing more mischief in an hour than a thousand monkeys would do in a day."[2]

For reasons unknown, in most cases such pandemonium seems to take place in the presence of a specific person, often a child, adolescent, or teenager. In past centuries it was believed that this may have been a result of witches casting spells on young people to curse their families. In more recent years, with the belief in witchcraft fading, some paranormal researchers believe that children are involved because poltergeists are unable to manifest their existence without what author A.R.G. Owen calls a "human focus."[3] Those who subscribe to this theory believe the poltergeists might be disembodied spirits using human agents as "mediums" to incarnate, or give themselves human form.

Other believers in the human agent theory say that certain individuals can create poltergeist phenomena without the presence of a ghost. They say the movement of objects, rapping, and other phenomena are traced to the agent's "astral" body, an invisible "energy" body said to reside within a

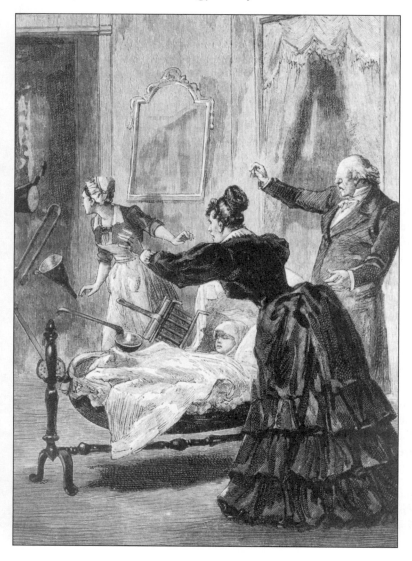

A baby sleeps as articles whirl around the room. Poltergeist activity often centers around a child or adolescent.

person that can move about independently as the "real" body stays behind. As Owen writes, "Poltergeist activities [may be] carried out by some invisible emanation, [an] 'astral body' or roving 'personality fragment' [that can break] off from the body or psyche of the poltergeist focus."[4]

Some paranormal researchers trace poltergeist activity to psychokinesis, or PK energy. This is a powerful blast of en-

The Antics of Poltergeists

When objects are moved by poltergeists, they are said to make odd trajectories that defy explanation. Writing in the early 1900s, psychic researcher William Barrett described this phenomena, quoted in *Ghosts and Poltergeists* by Herbert Thurston:

The movement of objects is usually quite unlike that due to gravitational or other attraction. They slide about, rise in the air, move in eccentric paths, sometimes in a leisurely manner, often turn round in their career, and usually descend quietly without hurting the observers. At other times an immense weight is lifted, often in daylight, no one being near, crockery is thrown about and broken, bedclothes are dragged off, the occupants sometimes lifted gently to the ground, and the bedstead tilted up or dragged about the room. The phenomena occur both in broad daylight and at night. Sometimes bells are continuously rung, even if all the bell wires are removed. Stones are frequently

thrown, but no one is hurt; I myself have seen a large pebble drop apparently from space in a room where the only culprit could have been myself, and certainly I did not throw it.

Objects disturbed by poltergeists seem to defy gravity, as shown in this engraving depicting items suspended from a ceiling.

ergy that is emitted, often unconsciously, from the mind, brain, or nervous system of a human agent. While this energy may be strong, it is uncontrollable; hence the chaotic results. This energy is often traced to adolescents who are under severe emotional stress. According to Gauld and Cornell, "[repressed] sexual feelings, repressed aggression, 'family tensions,' and hysteria have all been proposed, and . . . there is quite a lot of evidence to implicate plain fright. . . . I have not heard it claimed that a surfeit of happiness may cause a poltergeist outbreak."[5]

Whether a believer says poltergeist activity is from PK energy, astral bodies, or malicious ghosts or witches, no one has been able to explain how the basic laws of physics are suspended or reversed when large objects float or fly through space.

Showers of Stones

Despite the conflicting explanations, history is rife with detailed descriptions of poltergeist phenomena. Perhaps, not too surprisingly, many of these come from the distant past, a time when few people were literate and belief in ghosts, witches, and demons was widespread. One of the earliest cases took place in Bingem-am-Rhein, Germany, in A.D. 335, when stones flew through the air in the early hours of dawn, waking town residents as the stones allegedly crashed into their homes and through their walls and ceilings. While this occurrence might have been traced to a freak hailstorm or tornado, dirt and stone throwing events, known as "clodding," are among the most common types of poltergeist activity reported.

There is no answer as to how stones can pass through solid objects, such as walls and ceilings of houses. Little thought was given to scientific explanations, however, in the dozens of clodding incidents recorded in the seventeenth century. In 1682, for example, respected Boston reverend Increase Mather wrote about a shower of stones that rained against the walls and roof of a house belonging to George Walton. Mather describes the incident:

> Some of the people went [outdoors] . . . and stones came thick about them, sometimes falling down by them, sometimes touching them without any hurt done to them; though they seemed to come with great force, yet did no more but softly touch them; stones flying about the room, the doors being shut; the glass windows shattered to pieces by stones that seemed to come not from without but within, the lead of the glass casements, window bars etc. being driven forcibly outwards and so standing bent.[6]

Such descriptions were often published in pamphlets that were hungrily consumed by the public, and it is unknown if Mather embellished the story to make better reading. The story was also corroborated in a pamphlet published by a witness, Richard Chamberlain, who, as the secretary of the New Hampshire colony, was also a respected figure.

Another description of a stone-throwing poltergeist was published in Dortmund, Germany, little more than thirty years later. The event was recorded in the diary of Bethold Gerstmann, a respected doctor whose family was tormented for twenty-five days by a vengeful poltergeist. The clodding began on May 5, 1713, and was believed to be the work of naughty children or vagrants. After several windows were broken, members of the Gerstmann family stayed awake all night to watch for troublemakers. Although the stoning continued, the source of the objects could not be seen. In the eight days that followed, the house was forcefully bombarded by iron scraps, bricks, slate, and pottery fragments.

The poltergeist seemed to delight in shattering the glass and porcelain equipment in Gerstmann's laboratory. When family members picked up scientific instruments such as beakers and tubes to place them in cupboards, the instruments

In this drawing, poltergeists hurl bricks and stones, an activity characteristic of these mischievous spirits.

were shattered by stones even as they were held in their hands. Stones also passed through the pages of a Bible read by the eldest son. With joy, the poltergeist continued to infuriate the doctor, taking his valuable wig from a wall peg and plunging it into a pot of boiling water. When Gerstmann picked up a sword to slash futilely at his invisible tormentor, he found the sheath filled with dirt when he tried to replace the sword. Twenty-five days later, the haunting ended, as the family heard a voice announce "the end, the end today of mischief and stench."[7] As a final act of terror, clothing was mysteriously ripped off the body of the youngest son, a twelve-year-old who may have been the human agent in the haunting.

While the weird details of the Gerstmann poltergeist sound like they were invented by a prankster, Thurston writes:

> [It] is difficult to suppose they were pure invention. The Gerstmanns were people of some consequence who had nothing to gain by a fabrication of this sort. They professed to be devout Evangelicals, and as seems to have been the case with a dozen similar narratives preserved [from that era], their statement was really printed as an apologia. Such disturbances were then universally ascribed to the action of the devil and some degree of unpopularity was likely to be incurred by people who were unpleasantly mixed up with weird phenomena.[8]

Despite Thurston's assertion, clodding incidents are often blamed on children playing pranks. In a 1990s case in Druten, Holland, sand, stones, and chunks of dirt poured down on a family of Turkish immigrants when Çetin, their fifteen-year-old son, was near. When police were called, officers claimed Çetin was simply pulling a practical joke on his family. The officers recanted the charges, however, when they were driving the fifteen-year-old to a relative's house and were assaulted with sand and dirt while inside a moving automobile even as the young man had his hands in his pockets.

Spills and Messes

Teenagers are often present during other typical examples of poltergeist activity such as the movement of objects big

The Stone-Throwing Devil

In 1682, Richard Chamberlain, the secretary of the Province of New Hampshire, witnessed a typical poltergeist stone-throwing incident while staying at the home of George Mason in present-day New Castle, New Hampshire. He recorded his experience in a pamphlet entitled "Lithobolia: or, the Stone-Throwing Devil":

> [On] a Sunday Night, about Ten a Clock, many Stones were heard by my self, and the rest of the Family, to be thrown, and (with Noise) hit against the top and all sides of the House . . . by unseen Hands or Agents. . . . I was come down to them, having risen out of my Bed at this strange Alarm of all that were in the House, and . . . because there came many Stones, and those pretty great ones, some as big as my Fist, into the Entry or Porch of the House, we withdrew into the next Room to the Porch, no Person having receiv'd any Hurt. . . . Whilst we stood amazed at this Accident . . . we had many of these lapidary Salutations, but unfriendly ones; for, shutting the door, it was no small Surprise to me to have a good big Stone come with great force and noise (just by my Head) against the Door on the inside.

and small. While these events are traditionally blamed on ghosts, the first case traced to PK energy took place in Seaford, New York, on Long Island, in early 1958. This case was investigated by psychic researcher William Roll who was called by police when stationary objects began to move mysteriously about in the home of James Herrmann, his wife, and two children, thirteen-year-old Lucille, and twelve-year-old Jimmy.

Long Island police were first notified in February, when strange noises were heard in different rooms of the house before a bottle of holy water was found with its cap unscrewed, its contents spilled on a dresser in the master bedroom. A new, previously unopened bottle of perfume was also uncorked and dumped on the floor while bottles of shampoo and liquid medicine were spilled in the bathroom. Paint thinner was overturned in the cellar. The various messes were cleaned up and the bottles were set upright again. Soon a policeman arrived and assembled all members of the household in the living room. Even as this was taking place, the mysterious noises were heard again in the bathroom. When the officer investigated he found the shampoo spilled on the floor a second time. He noted that no tremors, wind, or other natural disturbances had taken place.

A detective named Joseph Tozzi was called to investigate and, as is typical in such cases, he blamed the children for playing practical jokes. Tozzi warned them that they would be severely punished for wasting his time. Despite the reprimand, the phenomena continued, even in Tozzi's presence. In one incident, a toy horse fell at the detective's feet after

In this 1958 photo, Detective Joseph Tozzi reads letters from people offering ideas about the source of the disturbances in the Herrmann household.

which the officer grilled Jimmy at length. This traumatized the entire family, as Tozzi wrote in his report: "[Jimmy] was sitting at the dining room table crying, Lucille was in the kitchen crying, and Mr. Herrmann was trying to bring some order to the house, as the complainant [Mrs. Herrmann] was also crying and on the verge of hysteria."[9]

The Poltergeist Liked Bottles

In the following weeks, the events at the Herrmann household seemed to intensify, as they often do in poltergeist cases. By March, tables were falling over and, on one occasion, a ceramic figurine of the Virgin Mary flew ten feet across the room and shattered with a loud crash. To ward off any more incidents, Mrs. Herrmann, a devout Catholic, placed many bottles of holy water around the house. However, as Roll writes in *The Poltergeist:*

> This was no help at all. In fact, it probably made matters worse: The Herrmann poltergeist liked bottles. There were 23 "bottle poppings," more than a third of the total number of occurrences. The bottles would loose their screw caps with an explosive sound, fall over, and spill their contents. . . . Five of the bottles were examined by the police laboratory. . . . There was no foreign matter, and the police were unable to come up with an explanation.[10]

As bottles continued to pop and fall over, investigators examined the house thoroughly. Building inspectors and structural, civil, and electrical engineers visited the home. They checked for malfunctions in the fuse box, the plumbing, the television, other electrical equipment, the oil heater, and the chimney. They even measured for unusual radio frequencies that could cause vibrations while employing a sensitive machine used to detect earthquakes. There were no malfunctions or tremors, and the events continued.

Finally, Roll pointed out that the incidents only occurred when Jimmy was home and awake. At first, investigators checked to see if Jimmy could have staged the incidents using magic tricks or scientific means, such as placing chemicals in the bottles to cause them to pop their tops. When this was ruled out, a psychiatrist was brought in to examine Jimmy. The doctor found that the boy had passive feelings of violence in general and hidden hostility toward his mother and father in particular. Roll, who was familiar with the alleged powers of PK energy, felt that subconscious anger caused the boy unconsciously to "focus" his energy to hurl objects in their general direction. As he writes in *Hauntings and Poltergeists:*

> There is little doubt that [Jimmy] was instrumental in bringing about the incidents in his home. It also seems clear that he was unaware of this. In fact it is uncertain if he ever saw an object start its movement. The occurrences appear to have been unconscious. The needs that seemed to be expressed in the incidents were unconscious as well but understandable in terms of [Jimmy's] personality. The objects that were disturbed, the nature of the incidents, and the directions of movements seemed to reflect the boy's relationship to significant others, in particular his parents. Isolation of affect may have inhibited the normal expression of his needs and facilitated RSPK.[11]

Poltergeist Pyromania

While bottle poppings and furniture tossing are rarely harmful, some poltergeists prefer to play more dangerous tricks, using fire. Since 1930, houses have spontaneously started on fire in Kentucky, Montana, Nova Scotia, and elsewhere after the poltergeist phenomena such as object moving and clodding have taken place.

When poltergeists burn things, there may be as many as a dozen fires breaking out within a few minutes. Such inci-

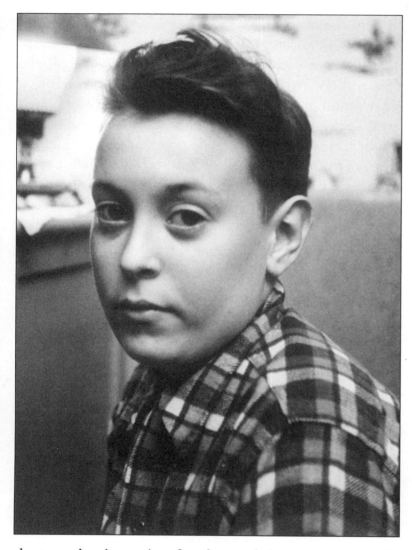

Psychic researcher William Roll concluded that poltergeist activity in the Herrmann house was the result of PK energy harnessed by young Jimmy (pictured).

dents tend to last only a few days and then stop as mysteriously as they began. People are rarely harmed as a result of the flames. As with other poltergeist activity, fire events often take place in the presence of a child. If the family moves after one house is burned, it may happen again in their next home. As D. Scott Rogo writes in *On the Track of the Poltergeist,* "If you ever hear about a poor family that just couldn't keep fires from breaking out in their house, keep the poltergeist well in mind."[12]

One case of poltergeist fires made the local television news in Simi Valley, California, in 1976. In this incident a man named John Eaton reported a series of small, unexplained fires breaking out in different places in his home during a short period of time. Unlike those involved in most poltergeist incidents, however, Eaton was unmarried and had no children. However, he did have a casual acquaintance known only as Fred who was about twenty years old. On the night of the fires, Fred and Eaton were drinking beer together, and Fred slept on the couch.

Poltergeist activity involving fire usually occurs in the presence of a child. The underside of this boy's mattress allegedly burned as he slept.

Trouble began when the kitchen table burst into flames at 3 A.M. After Eaton woke to the smell of smoke and dragged

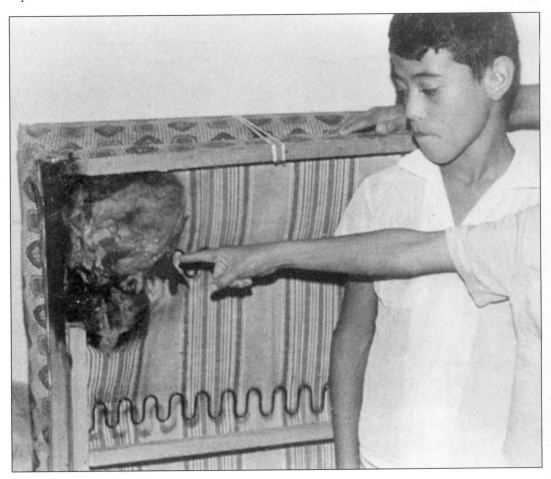

the table out into the backyard, he returned to the house to find his bed was on fire. This caused the man to rush to the backyard, pick up the garden hose, and extinguish the fire by spraying the hose through an open window. Fred, mysteriously, remained asleep. However, the couch where he lay was next to go up in flames. Eaton woke Fred by spraying him— and the couch—with the garden hose. Over the course of the next fifteen minutes, Eaton and Fred extinguished several more spontaneous furniture fires that seemed to move in a straight line through the house.

Firefighters belatedly arrived on the scene and after talking to the men, investigators concluded that Eaton or Fred had purposely started the fires. While the fire department let the matter go, paranormal researchers concluded that Fred was the cause of the fires, even though at age twenty he was a little old to be what Rogo calls a "poltergeist child."[13] Nonetheless, there seemed to be no other explanation. As to why and how such a phenomenon takes place, Owen attempts to explain:

> It could be imagined that the same force [that moves objects] could raise the temperature of a solid by producing an increase in the molecular agitation within it. When hot enough in the presence of air it would ignite. . . . [The] argument may be of utility in suggesting how fire-raising *could* be included in the normal repertoire of the classical poltergeist.[14]

While Owen's theory may explain how objects start on fire, it fails to address another phenomenon: flaming matches that appear out of thin air. In a case from 1886, Willie Brough, a twelve-year-old California boy, caused fires of this type. According to the San Francisco *Bulletin,* "There were five fires at his school, one in the center of the ceiling, one in the teacher's desk, one in her wardrobe, and two on the wall."[15] Because of the evidence left behind by burning matches,

Brough was expelled from school even though he called attention to the fires, which indicates he did not set them purposely. More tragically, Brough's parents believed the boy was possessed by the devil and threw him out of the house; he was never heard from again.

Sometimes poltergeist fires can simply burn in the presence of a human agent. On the Caribbean island of Antigua in the Bahamas, a teenage girl named Lilly White was able to manifest flames directly from her skin. The fires hovered a few inches above her and caused her no harm. Although the story was published in the *New York Times* in 1929, there has been no explanation for White's combustible condition.

Puddles, Damp Spots, and Slime

While fires often terrify their victims, poltergeists have also been said to play with water. This was the case reported in the Lawrence, Massachusetts *Eagle-Tribune* in October 1963. An unnamed family first noticed a strange, slimy damp spot on the wall of their apartment. Moments later, a loud pop like a firecracker was heard, and a strong jet of water shot from the wall. Although the apartment supervisor was called immediately to shut off the apartment's water supply, the event continued for three days, destroying the apartment and the family's belongings.

A case of a water poltergeist taking over several houses at once was recorded in the small town of Scherfede, Germany, in October 1972. At first, small damp spots formed on walls and in the carpet of one family's house. Workmen were called but could find no problems with the plumbing. The water spots continued to appear for several months, but on December 10, it seems a poltergeist attacked the entire neighborhood. Psychic researcher Hans Bender describes this strange event:

> In intervals of 20–30 minutes, big water puddles appeared in the drawing room of the house. The family

The Poltergeist That Played the Drum

Poltergeists often terrorize their victims with loud sounds, but few have been as creative as the mysterious poltergeist of Tedworth, England, that allegedly beat on a drum and practiced other violence against the town's magistrate. The antics of the drumming spirit were published on the "The Gazetteer of Mysterious Britain" Web site:

In March, 1661 John Mompesson of Tedworth brought a suit against a gypsy drummer whom he charged with fraud. He was released but his drum was confiscated and given to Mompesson. Within hours the drum had levitated itself and began to be beaten by phantom hands—days of endless drumming followed and eventually the magistrate had the drum destroyed. However the drumming continued and poltergeist activity began in earnest with objects being thrown by some invisible agency and people being lifted into the air. It drummed on the bed of the children, threw shoes and wrestled with the servants. It purred like a cat, beat the children's legs black and blue, put a spike into Mr. Mompesson's bed, and a knife into his mother's, hid a Bible under the grate and turned money black in people's pockets. . . . After a year exactly, the poltergeist ceased its disturbance and never returned.

[known only as] K.—father, mother and a 13-year-old girl Kerstin—heard a splashing when they were in another room. Nothing happened when they were present, and no one had even seen a pool in formation. Technicians came and admitted that they were completely puzzled and could not find any cause. Trickery was excluded by carefully observing the room in question. At 7:30 P.M. neighbors of the next [door] house came and asked for help: floods of water had suddenly appeared on the second floor and were coming down the staircase. There was too much to mop up with floor cloths. Helpers formed [a mop brigade] and brushed it out of the house. They were still at work when an hour later help was claimed for the next house where unexplainable water pools and splashes appeared and, another hour later, the same happened in the adjoining house, the last one of the row. This continued, more or less intensely, for three days. [16]

High Tides and Rainfall

Although there is no definitive explanation for the water events allegedly created by poltergeists, they may have been caused by fissures in the earth or other natural phenomena. Psychic researcher G.W. Lambert has developed a theory that follows this line of thinking, saying strange noises, vibrating

Poltergeists sometimes play tricks with water. In this photo, researchers check the plumbing of a house that has experienced poltergeist activity.

floors, moving furniture, and other oddities commonly associated with poltergeists might be related to the shifting earth rather than restless spirits. Owen explains this theory:

> Lambert . . . suggested that noises and vibrations of buildings are often caused by water moving in subterranean rivers or sewers. Under special conditions of high tide, blocking of outlets by silting up, or excessive rainfall, these underground channels contain water, or even compressed air, at high pressure. This may result in the "jacking up" and subsequent [settling] of a building, with resultant "cracking" or other noises. In a series of papers he has collected data tending to show correlation between auditory haunting and (a) proximity to tidal regions, (b) winter rather than summer, (c) rainfall, (d) local geology, particularly provenance of limestone, (e) the state of the tides.[17]

Lambert based his theories on a study done of an allegedly haunted house near the sea in Buckinghamshire, England. Investigation showed that there was an old sewer beneath the house that shifted during rising tides and strong rainfalls. It was also discovered that the house was built near the site of an earthquake fault subject to mild tremors. Others dispute this theory, and in cases such as the one in Seaford, investigators searched for underground sewers, mild earthquakes, and other natural causes. While no poltergeist incidents have been captured on film, there is no shortage of alleged events associated with ghosts, PK energy, or some other mysterious force. As to their cause, most cases remain unsolved.

Chapter 2

Poltergeists, Possession, and Exorcism

It is a common notion among parapsychologists that poltergeist events can be traced to teenagers who may be utilizing psychokinesis, or PK energy, to move objects. There are those who believe, however, that human agents of poltergeists are possessed by supernatural agents, and their bodies and actions are controlled without their consent.

Poltergeist possession is said to be a terrifying experience both for the victim and the friends and family of the possessed. Those said to be possessed by poltergeists are often troubled by severe headaches, insomnia, buzzing in the ears, hallucinations, and even insanity. They might utter strange, unintelligible sounds in voices not their own. Other symptoms include levitation, or floating into the air, and regurgitation of strange objects such as feathers, leaves, and dirt. Although the victims have no control over these bizarre actions, they are often all too aware that the events are happening. Sometimes the trauma is so great, however, that the possessed will block out any memories and will remember nothing.

"Shadows of the Demon"

In the past, a person said to be possessed by a poltergeist was often said to be under a witch's or devil's curse. Raymond Bayless explains in *The Enigma of the Poltergeist:*

> The destructive aspect so often encountered [with poltergeists] fitted into the demonic framework, and . . . the actions of objects paranormally moved were plainly under the control of satanic forces. The very concept of supernormal forces and actions [such as PK energy] belonged to the future, and there only remained the explanation of witchcraft. The existence of subconscious activity was unknown. Either things were acted on by the known, normal forces, or they were influenced by magical means. Magic was equated with the black art. . . . The poltergeist—and hauntings—were shadows of the demon.[18]

The Flying Saint

In past centuries, the devil was often blamed for poltergeist activities. However, many religious figures were also allegedly the focus of strange phenomena. In these cases, events were attributed to possession by heavenly powers. In *Poltergeists* Sacheverell Sitwell describes the bizarre phenomena surrounding seventeenth-century Italian St. Joseph of Copertino:

In his eighth year St. Joseph of Copertino had an ecstatic vision while at school, and this was renewed several times. . . . At an adult age . . . he joined the priesthood. It was then that his miracles began. Frequently he would be raised from his feet and be suspended in the air. For thirty-five years he was not allowed to attend choir, go to the refectory, walk in procession, or say Mass, but was ordered to remain in his room, where a private chapel was prepared for him. These strictures were put upon him owing to the excitement caused by his appearance, and the anticipation of some feat of levitation on his part. . . . He is reputed to have flown upon seventy occasions in all; he hovered for a quarter of an hour over the high altar; flew over the heads of the congregation in the presence of the Spanish ambassador; and, upon occasion, flew with other persons whom he caught up by the hair, or round the waist.

In the seventeenth century, fear of demons reached epic proportions in Salem Village, Massachusetts. Over a period of several months between December 1691 and September 1692, over one hundred innocent villagers were accused of witchcraft or worshipping demons. At least nineteen were hung from the neck until dead on Gallows Hill. Some who have studied the evidence, however, believe that strange events in the town might have actually been caused by poltergeists.

The witch hysteria began when about a dozen young girls accused their neighbors of pinching, scratching, and biting them. Mather wrote about one such incident concerning accused witch George Burroughs: "Biting was one of the ways which the witches used for vexing the sufferers; when they cried out of G.B. [George Burroughs] Biting them, the print of the Teeth would be seen on the Flesh of the Complainers."[19]

Between December 1691 and September 1692, some nineteen innocent residents of the village of Salem, Massachusetts, were hanged on suspicion of practicing witchcraft.

These poltergeist events were often accompanied by loud unearthly noises also associated with poltergeists. One such incident was described by Deodat Lawson in *Narratives of the Witchcraft Cases 1648–1706* edited by George Lincoln Burr:

> [The accused witch's] motions did produce like effect as to . . . Pinching, Bruising, Tormenting [them]. . . . [The afflicted girl] had a grievous Fit . . . so that there was such an hideous scrietch [screech] and noise . . . as did amaze me. [20]

Further evidence of poltergeist possession is traced to the girls who were adolescents and teenagers, the typical ages of poltergeist agents. As in many other poltergeist cases, the children were extremely repressed by religious and social customs that did not allow them to express feelings of joy, rebelliousness, and anger.

While the symptoms of the afflicted girls have been blamed on witchcraft, demons, and poltergeist possession, there is little proof that it was anything more than group hysteria. As Bayless writes, however, well-known "cases of [demonic] possession are difficult to distinguish from a certain class of poltergeist outbreak . . . and in a great part [both] must originate from the same source." [21]

In this courtroom scene from Salem, adolescent girls writhe in fits that many villagers attributed to demonic possession.

Foaming at the Mouth

In the nineteenth century Hélène Poirier, a resident of Paris, was another victim who seemed to suffer both from demonic and poltergeist possession. Poirier's problems began in 1850 with typical poltergeist activity. She was awakened in the middle of the night by rapping and pounding at such a volume that the neighbors thought guns were being fired. A few months later, Poirier's body froze into a rigid position so unnatural doctors concluded she was possessed by a demon. These symptoms continued off and on for years.

In August 1867, one of the stranger incidents occurred when a number of people claimed to see Poirier levitate and float several feet above her bed. Like the afflicted girls in Salem, the woman also suffered violent pinches, bites, slaps, kicks, and hair pulling thought to be caused by a poltergeist. During these fits, Poirier was able to carry on conversations in Greek and Latin, two languages she was unfamiliar with in her normal conscious state.

During her most severe torments, Poirier became violent, foaming at the mouth, cursing God, and calling for the devil. As with poltergeist events, furniture and other objects flew about the room and horrible noises assaulted the ears of witnesses. Although priests tried to perform exorcisms to cure the woman, Poirier remained tormented by her demons until her death in 1914.

Skeptics have attributed cases such as Poirier's to medical problems. For example, those with a disease called disseminated sclerosis suffer from spastic jerking and extremely rigid joints. Some people with Tourette's syndrome yell profanities and obscenities and make grunts, barks, curses, yelps, snorts, and sniffs. They also display tics, foot stomping, and facial contortions that appear suddenly and just as suddenly cease. While these problems can be controlled today by modern medicine, in the past many people suffering from illnesses with similar symptoms, such as Huntington's chorea, schizophrenia, and Parkinson's disease, were accused of being possessed by poltergeists or the devil.

A Merry and Amused Poltergeist

While the exact cause of Poirier's problems has never been found, her case was known to Allan Kardec, a French spiritualist who surely attributed the woman's problems to ghostly possession. Kardec believed that bodiless, or disincarnate, spirits wandered the earth waiting for reincarnation, that is,

Allan Kardec, a nineteenth-century French spiritualist, believed that lost spirits waiting to be reborn sometimes possessed living bodies.

rebirth of their souls into a living body. Sometimes these disincarnate souls inhabited human beings and caused mischief commonly associated with poltergeists. Kardec published his beliefs in *The Spirits' Book* in 1856, after conducting séances in which he went into a trance and allegedly talked to such spirits.

Four years after Kardec published his book, there was a boisterous disturbance blamed on poltergeists in a Paris home on the Rue des Noyers. Every window of the home was smashed, furniture was overturned and destroyed, and objects that the residents had never seen before were thrown about the house. Eventually the pandemonium drove the residents from their home. The source of trouble was blamed on a young maid who worked in the house. Kardec decided to hold a séance to converse with the spirits and determine the cause of the problems.

Kardec claims to have called up the Rue des Noyers poltergeist who was infuriated at being disturbed. The spirit allegedly questioned Kardec angrily: "Why do you call on me? Do you want to have some stones thrown at you?"[22] Kardec asked the spirit why it created chaos in the house on Rue des Noyers. The spirit replied, "For I am merry and like to amuse myself sometimes."[23] When Kardec asked if it used a human helper to trash the house, the spirit said that it certainly did; he possessed the maidservant who was unaware that it was working through her. Kardec asked the poltergeist how it used the maid, and the spirit, implying that it was able to utilize what is now called PK energy, answered: "I helped myself through the electric nature of the girl, joined to my own . . . thus we were able to transport objects between us."[24]

Upon further questioning, the spirit told Kardec that it was once a human being, a rag picker who was able to stay drunk most of the time by selling discarded scraps of cloth to buy cheap wine. The rag picker lived on Rue des Noyers and was constantly harassed and ridiculed by residents of the street. After he died, he decided to return to his former street, take possession of someone, and create havoc among the inhabitants in order to entertain himself.

Those who believe in the mischievous poltergeist of Rue des Noyers judge Kardec on his word. They point out that he was a founding figure of the French spiritualist movement, which swept across the Western world in the following years. Others say that Kardec was a charlatan who made up stories to help generate fame and sell more books. Since the maidservant never told her version of the story, the possessive poltergeist seems to have had the final word on the rampage on Rue des Noyers.

An Act of the Devil?

Although the rag picker poltergeist was simply out to have some fun, such disturbances are often associated with the devil. In many cases, instead of calling a spiritualist, victims of poltergeists use the Bible, the cross, and other religious symbols to drive away the perceived demon. Oftentimes religious officials are called to perform an exorcism, a ritual that utilizes incantations, commands, or prayer in order to force the evil spirit to stop afflicting the living. These events have mixed results. Sometimes the poltergeist is emboldened by the exorcism and its behavior becomes more violent. Other times the poltergeist's activities cease. Since poltergeist hauntings are said to last for only short periods of time in any case, it is not known if the exorcisms make any difference.

A case of a religious battle with a poltergeist was recorded in the household of A.S. Pillay, a magistrate in a town in Tanjore, India. Pillay reported that on March 3, 1920, a typical poltergeist haunting began in his home when spontaneous fires broke out over the period of about thirty minutes. The fires burned silk clothing belonging to various women of the household, and restarted several times after they were

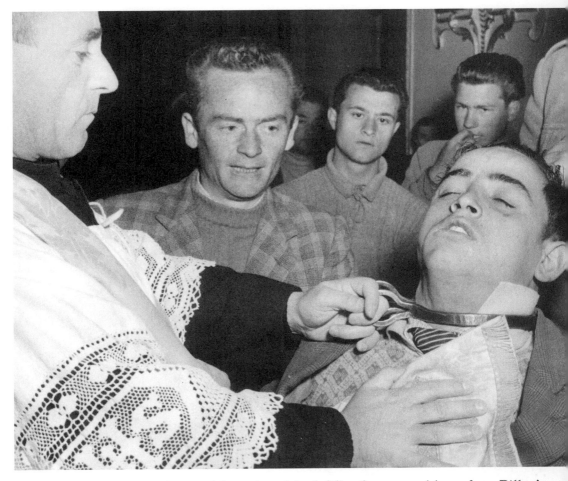

In this photo from 1950, an Italian priest performs an exorcism with special implements designed to expel the poltergeist that has been tormenting this man.

thoroughly extinguished. The fires were blamed on Pillay's teenage daughter who was given a beating. When the fires continued the next day, this time burning the kitchen curtains, Pillay wrote, "This created a suspicion that it was the act of [the] devil."[25]

To counteract the disturbance, Pillay, a Christian, hung pictures of the Sacred Heart, the Virgin Mary, and other saints in every room of his home. With chalk in hand, he drew crosses on walls, doors, and entryways to his yard. This seemed to amuse Pillay's poltergeist who started the pictures on fire and smeared the crosses with cow dung. One particularly large picture in a glass frame of St. Margaret Mary was removed from the wall and smashed to bits. Pillay relates what happened next:

> Seeing the devilish troubles I took a standing crucifix made of black wood . . . and placed it [on] the [mantelpiece] by the side of the hearth. I myself sat about three feet to the north and was reciting the Apostles' Creed over and over. Within a second the crucifix was missing. To my great grief and extreme sorrow I found the crucifix in the fire and the wood was burning. None else was there except me.[26]

Undaunted, Pillay erected several other crucifixes that either disappeared or were destroyed. Similarly, the victim continued to draw around his home and yard crosses that were continually smeared with dung, often moments after they were created.

A Tug-of-War with the Devil

Pillay soon brought a local priest to examine his home and hear his strange story. As the men were eating lunch, the poltergeist initiated new tactics, dropping a clay pot full of milk from the ceiling and levitating pans full of rice, sauce, and buttermilk into the air before smashing them down onto the floor.

On the advice of the priest, the Pillay family moved into a new residence. No sooner had they arrived than they found two broomsticks burning. Several newly purchased clay cooking vessels were broken. As Pillay writes, the poltergeist even tried to grab pots out of the hands of family members:

> My daughter's husband took hold of the rice vessel and there was a regular tug-of-war between him and the devil, the former seizing the vessel very strongly and the latter trying with great force to snatch away the vessel with rice inside from the hold of my son-in-law.[27]

Fraud and Deception

In many cases of alleged poltergeist possession, skeptical investigators sometimes find that mischievous children, not spirits, are responsible. On the "Exorcism! Driving Out the Nonsense" Web site, Joe Nickell elaborates:

> Trickery was behind the poltergeist-like disturbances of 1848 that launched modern spiritualism. As the Fox Sisters confessed

decades later, their pretended spirit contact began as the pranks of "very mischievous children" who, Margaret Fox explained, began their shenanigans "to terrify our dear mother, who was a very good woman and very easily frightened" and who "did not suspect us of being capable of a trick because we were so young." The schoolgirls threw slippers at a disliked brother-in-law, shook the dinner table, and produced noises by bumping the floor with an apple on a string and by knocking on the bedstead. . . .

> The Fox Sisters were followed in 1854 by the Davenport Brothers, schoolboys Ira and William, who were the focus of cutlery that danced about the family's kitchen table, and other odd events. . . . Soon the boys advanced to spirit-rapped messages, "trance" writing and speaking, and other "spirit manifestations." In his old age, Ira confessed . . . that the brothers' spirit communications—which launched and maintained their careers as two of the world's best-known spiritualistic mediums—had all been produced by trickery. Indeed, they had been caught in deceptions many times.

A doctor shows how one of the Fox Sisters faked poltergeist noises by cracking her knee.

Following this incident, the family was forced to use unbreakable brass pots that were secured to the legs of furniture with strong rope.

After several chaotic days, the evil poltergeist purportedly began to leave written messages to the terrified family, warning them: "My name is Rajamadan [chief mischief maker]. I will not leave you. . . . If you don't run away from this house, I would recommend you to my goddess for punishment. . . . Don't you know that I am the King? I will not leave this house."[28]

When Pillay's problems continued, he consulted with three Catholic priests who advised that he begin a regimen

This photo shows a message allegedly written by a sixteenth-century ghost on the floor of a living room in an English house.

of extended prayer. As in traditional exorcisms, Pillay commanded the spirit to leave his home, saying:

> You devil, why do you trouble us like this? You know very well that we are all the children of God and we have not done anything wrong to you. . . . Your proper place is hell, where there would always be burning fire. It would be well and good if you would go back to your place.[29]

At that point, Pillay claims the poltergeist lifted a large, burning log from the hearth and threw it at him, briefly starting the rug on fire. The battle ensued for days as Pillay directed intense and prolonged prayers to St. Joseph. During the exorcism, Pillay was hit, burned, had objects thrown at him, and saw crucifixes and other items destroyed. With the help of a Catholic priest the praying seemed to help, however. On March 19, more than two weeks after the troubles began, the poltergeist was exorcized, purportedly leaving a message on the bathroom wall that it was taking its leave.

Pillay may have believed that his prayers exorcized the poltergeist, but there is doubt among religious experts that such exorcisms can work. As Catholic writer Sir Shane Leslie explains: "Exorcism is aimed at Satan and a poltergeist is on a lower or say less sinister level."[30] This allegedly leaves poltergeists less susceptible to religious cures.

The Devil in Daly City

For believers in PK energy, poltergeist activity with demonic overtones may be traced to the deep psychological conflicts victims have over their religious beliefs. Although it may seem that a demon is creating havoc, it may be the victim's repressed religious feelings unconsciously emitting PK energy with weird and frightening results. In some cases, a formal exorcism may reassure the victim and end the problem. This was the case in 1972 in Daly City, California.

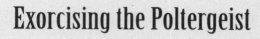

Exorcising the Poltergeist

Many modern researchers believe that poltergeist activities are caused by unhappy people who unconsciously emit powerful PK energy. This causes fires and loud noises, makes objects fly, and so on. Those hoping for a cure may try exorcism. As Raymond Bayless writes in *The Enigma of the Poltergeist,* the power of suggestion central to exorcism can help end the attacks if the human agent has a religious background:

> In spite of the fundamental mystery that shrouds the enigma of the poltergeist, certain . . . suggestions and explanations can be advanced which do shed some . . . light upon the mechanisms behind the ghostly force's response to exorcism. One obvious clue is the great part played by subconscious activity.

Generally malicious and frequently destructive outbursts of phenomena have been traced to unhappiness, resentment, frustration, and tensions in general existing within [a person creating poltergeist activity]. . . .

The key to controlling this force through exorcism is suggestion. The necessary forms of suggestion capable of modifying and even ending these psychological [eruptions] are easily found. They lie within social traditions, and perhaps most important of all, within the compass of religion. I believe a general rule may be stated . . . that custom and religious beliefs are established within the unconscious, so . . . the phenomena of the poltergeist [may] be subject to exorcism.

Problems began as spontaneous fires broke out in the home of a young couple, Jan and Brian Neven, and their newborn son Stephen. Objects were hurled through the air or disappeared, only to be found in a different place later on. Activities increased when, on several occasions, the couple felt as if they were being beaten, sometimes so severely that they were hurled to the ground. The problems followed the Nevens to another home and then to a motel.

Psychic investigators were called in and noted that the activities began when Brian, an Orthodox Jew, was in the process of converting to Catholicism, the religion practiced by his wife. The hauntings were also tied to baby Stephen, who was born around the time the conversion began. In fact, the baby quickly became the focus of the poltergeist, evoking a deep sense of terror in the young family. In one incident, a fire started in the baby's brand-new crib, reducing the crib to ashes. Days later a crucifix was found in a most un-likely place, as investigator Freda Morris writes:

> I had been carrying the baby around the house for about 20 minutes, when suddenly he began to cry so loud that I returned him to Brian. He and Jan took the baby into the bedroom to change his diaper. Almost as soon as they entered the bedroom Jan screamed and we all rushed after them. Jan said the baby had started to shake and his eyes had rolled back into his head. When I touched him he was damp and cold but his eyes were focused and he was quiet. Jan went ahead with changing his diaper and when she took it off we all saw twined around his genitals a necklace with a cross which had disappeared from Jan's neck two hours earlier. The young mother fainted and the baby began to cry again.[31]

The necklace made more appearances over the course of the next several days. It was found wrapped around the baby's leg moments before a Bible started on fire. The attacks picked up in intensity as the poltergeist hurled eggs at Stephen and wrapped his blankets tightly around his face, nearly suffo-cating him. Family members were choked, slapped, bruised, and knocked unconscious by invisible blows.

In one attempt at communication with the poltergeist, Brian left a pad and pen on a kitchen table. Later that night he came back to find the threatening words "he, child, die, baby, back, baby, stay."[32] Taking little comfort in this statement, the Nevens called several priests, mediums, and paranormal in-vestigators, but found no solace in their words. Believing that the devil was the cause of their troubles, the family asked Father Karl Pazelt, a Greek Orthodox Catholic priest, to conduct an exorcism. Over the next few months, Pazelt conducted an in-credible fourteen exorcisms in the Nevens' home. This seemed to work, and the hauntings stopped.

While some say the Daly City poltergeist was a demon, psychic researcher Rogo blames the incident on one or both of the baby's parents. In *The Poltergeist Experience: Investigations into Ghostly Phenomena,* Rogo writes:

> Brian was Jewish, his wife was Catholic, and Brian converted to Catholicism during the period of poltergeistery. This indicates that the Nevens were experiencing an intense religious crisis in their personal lives at the time. When I first read of the case I remembered something I had learned while taking a course in marriage counseling. I had been instructed that the time of greatest potential family strife in Jewish-Catholic marriages, especially when the wife is Catholic, is the birth of a baby. Although mutually respecting each other's beliefs, couples often encounter severe emotional problems at this time, since each may consciously or unconsciously desire that the

Psychic investigator Guy Playfair examines the roof of a house in Brazil where poltergeist activity purportedly took place. Psychic investigators often study poltergeist cases.

baby be brought up in his or her own religion. This occurs even if neither of them is particularly devout and can cause irreparable damage to some marriages. During the Daly City poltergeist, the baby was the focus of the assaults. Could the poltergeist have been an outlet for hidden conflicts over the child? Could assaults on it have represented a means by which the Nevens "punished" the baby for being the root of the conflict? [33]

It is possible that this intense conflict was resolved when the prolonged exorcism subconsciously resolved Brian and Jan's psychological conflicts. With their minds at ease, the spontaneous PK energy events simply stopped.

Lukewarm Wickedness

It is often confusing to examine poltergeist phenomena in the context of exorcism and possession. In most cases, those troubled by a poltergeist are religious people. It is natural for them to assume that the unexplainable activity is somehow tied to the devil—and that the way to repel it is by praying or brandishing religious symbols. However, as psychic investigator Guy Playfair warns in *This House Is Haunted,* "Prayers can be effective, but only when said with real sincerity. Mumbling ritual phrases in the general direction of God is no good at all. You have to mean what you're saying." [34]

Praying may be a normal reaction to an abnormal situation, but some believe that poltergeists are confused ghosts of the dead caught between this world and the afterlife. While they may take physical possession of victims and destroy the crosses and Bibles waved at them, they are not nearly as malevolent as Satan is said to be. The poltergeists might traumatize their victims, but rarely leave any lasting damage. As Gauld and Cornell write: "If poltergeist phenomena are the work of discarnate non-human spirits, those spirits must surely be ones thus lukewarm in wickedness." [35]

Chapter 3

Hunting Poltergeists

M ost people instinctively run away from poltergeists, terrified by the peculiar and unexplainable activities. However, some are intent on finding answers to poltergeist hauntings, and instead of fleeing, they move into homes where such activities are taking place. In doing so they risk their own physical and mental well-being to help victims solve their ghostly dilemmas. While many of these paranormal investigators labor in obscurity, a few have become relatively well known, mostly from the books they have published about their activities.

Most researchers are not driven by a desire for fame but a need to prove with solid scientific evidence why poltergeist activities take place. These people, commonly referred to as psychic investigators, employ a variety of methods, both scientific and supernatural, in order to follow and trace the movements of poltergeists.

Poltergeist hunters either work for a fee or volunteer their services to those who believe that they are victims of mischievous hauntings. While there have always been scholars who investigated hauntings, the first people to call themselves ghost hunters began to appear in the nineteenth century when the fascination with apparitions was at its peak in the United States and Europe. Many of these people, then called spiritualists, were charlatans or fakers who staged poltergeist events using hidden partners, wires, and other tricks to create loud

Ghosts or Poltergeists?

It is only in the past fifty years or so that poltergeist activity has been traced to psychokinesis, or PK energy emanating from a human agent. Before that, poltergeist incidents were usually thought of as ghost hauntings. However, as William Roll writes in *The Poltergeist,* there are distinct differences between ghosts and poltergeists:

> [Ghostly] disturbances can generally be divided into either of two groups: Haunting and poltergeist phenomena. . . . In general, poltergeist incidents are connected with an individual, while hauntings seem to be connected with an area, usually a house. Physical disturbances predominate in poltergeist incidents, hallucinatory experiences in hauntings. These [latter] experiences, which may include seeing ghosts and hearing footsteps, are called hallucinatory because they are generally experienced by some persons and not by others. . . .
>
> Haunting occurrences may also involve physical disturbances, but these instances of apparent RSPK are generally less frequent and violent than in poltergeist cases. However, hauntings tend to stretch over longer periods of time. Poltergeist disturbances are usually of fairly short duration, rarely lasting more than a couple of months, while a haunting may go on for years. As a rule, there seems to be no (living) person around whom haunting incidents revolve.

noises, make tables float, spread puddles on the floor, and so on.

In England there were so many such frauds in the poltergeist hunting business that, in 1882, the Society for Psychical Research (SPR) published official guidelines that legitimate ghost hunters were told to follow. This information is explained by Katherine Ramsland in *Ghost: Investigating the Other Side:*

> The SPR categorized possible [poltergeist] manifestations in terms of information received: noises, odors, physical contact, movement of an object, and appearances. They urged investigators to be open but skeptical, and to check everything. Sites had to be investigated under many conditions, during both the day and night. Maps are checked for things in the area that might be causing the apparent manifestation [such as underground sewers]. . . . Then eyewitness accounts are recorded. [36]

Tools of the Poltergeist Hunter

An honest investigator intent on proving the existence of a poltergeist has several techniques for determining if a disincarnate spirit is present. For example, a psychic researcher might draw chalk rings around furniture and objects on tables to determine if anything has been moved by unseen energy or a spirit. A good description of this activity comes from renowned ghost hunter Harry Price's investigation at the Borley Rectory, described in *The Most Haunted House in England:*

> [We] "ringed" with coloured chalks every movable object in the house. In addition, we placed a number

Ghost hunter Harry Price draws chalk rings around vases to determine whether they move during a poltergeist investigation.

of small objects about the place: match-box, cigarette carton, and small odds and ends. These we very carefully and accurately ringed in order to inform us, or future observers, whether any force—normal or paranormal—had moved them.[37]

While Price used boxes and cartons, investigators may also "load" a site with items meant to provoke a poltergeist. These articles may include religious symbols, toys, small knives, or playing cards, all of which have been allegedly thrown according to eyewitnesses of poltergeist incidents. Investigators leave sound-activated tape recorders around loaded sites to pick up unusual sounds.

Sometimes a simple battery-powered bell and a few wires can instantly alert poltergeist hunters that objects have been moved. In October 1937, Dr. D.F. Bellamy visited the Borley Rectory to conduct an experiment in hopes of recording poltergeist activity. Bellamy hooked an electric bell to some wire contacts taped to a pile of books that were surrounded by chalk marks. If the books were moved or disturbed, the electrical switch, or contact breaker, would make the bell ring, notifying the ghost hunters of activity. Professor Bellamy described his experiment:

> At 12.10 A.M. [we] were quietly watching . . . sitting on the floor with our backs to the wall, and the moon was streaming in at the window. [We] sat there until 12.50 A.M. when . . . [the electric] bell in circuit with contact breaker under pile of books on marble mantelpiece in living room . . . started ringing and continued to ring for the space of about a minute, when it ceased abruptly. . . . Now, on our arrival in the room, *the books were displaced, no book occupying its original position,* and the bottom one was right off the contact breaker. The window of the room was found to be sealed. . . . Nothing else in the room was disturbed. In view of the displacement of the books we are quite unable to account for this phenomenon. . . . The ringing was a very startling

experience. . . . Knowing something about the vagaries of electrical contacts, I should not have attached much importance to the incident had the books not been so greatly displaced and the apparatus moved out of the chalk marks. The fact that it ceased so suddenly also added to our bewilderment.[38]

A thermograph records a sudden, unexplained drop in temperature in a house in France, indicating a possible poltergeist presence.

In addition to bells, weather recording instruments are also extremely helpful to a poltergeist hunter. Tools to measure atmospheric pressure, wind force, and humidity can all register disturbances allegedly traced to poltergeist movements. Thermometers are among the best tools for investigators since poltergeist activity is reported to cause room temperatures to dip rapidly. A psychic researcher will own as many as several dozen thermometers and place them all over a suspected haunt site, including out-of-the-way spots such as chimney stacks, closets, attics, crawl spaces, and basements. These are checked on a continuous patrol throughout an investigation. Instruments called thermographs, while expensive, are particularly useful as they automatically produce a graph showing detailed temperature fluctuations over a specific period.

Some detection instruments are much more low-tech, however. In cases where strange puddles of water appear, investigators have used divining rods, forked sticks held with both hands that are said to point to the ground where there is subterranean water. In addition, many poltergeist hunters assemble a kit suggested by Price:

> Into a large suitcase are packed the following articles: A pair of soft felt overshoes used for creeping, unheard, about the house in order that neither human beings nor paranormal 'entities' shall be disturbed when producing 'phenomena'; steel measuring tape for measuring rooms, passages, testing the thickness of walls in looking for secret chambers or hidey-holes; steel screw-eyes . . . sealing tool, strong cord or tape, and adhesive surgical tape, for sealing doors, windows or cupboards . . . [coil] of electric [wire], small electric bells, dry batteries and switches (for secret electrical contacts); . . . a small portable telephone for communicating with assistant in another part of building or garden; notebook, red, blue and black pencils;

Mind-Reading Poltergeists

Poltergeist researchers must beware not to make a situation worse by giving the spirit any new ideas. On the Web site "Ghost Club Talk: John Spencer On Poltergeists," John Spencer, a member of the Ghost Club in the United Kingdom, explains how this may happen:

> Two types of "contagion" have been noted in poltergeist cases. One type is where a poltergeist seems to acquire ideas from investigators in a property. For example, an investigator may mention a rare type of phenomena which may have occurred in another case at another location, perhaps years before. Soon after the poltergeist starts to imitate the earlier phenomena, even if investigators have not mentioned it to any other person in the property. This suggests that poltergeists have an ability to read minds. Certainly the way in which they succeed in avoiding detection and actually being seen in action suggests a telepathic ability of knowing when the observer's attention is elsewhere.

sketching block and case of drawing instruments for making plans; bandages, iodine and a flask of brandy in case member of investigating staff or resident is injured or faints; ball of string, stick of chalk, matches, electric [flashlight] and candle; bowl of mercury for detecting tremors in room or passage.[39]

"Five Tons of Equipment"

A poltergeist investigator might also pack miniature video cameras and motion detectors to sense alleged poltergeist activity. In the twenty-first century, a new array of high-tech gadgets are used to make the invisible visible. Instruments that were formerly available only to the police and military, such as night vision scopes, are now part of a modern hunter's tool kit. Other modern tools are used to detect the subtle electrical charges to the air, known as electromagnetic frequencies, or EMFs. These frequencies may account for percipients reporting that their hair stood on end or their skin tingled because a spirit was said to be present. To document this phenomenon—and detect the presence of a poltergeist—psychic investigators use sensitive electronic instruments such as gauss meters, EMF meters, and radio frequency counters. Sometimes these gauges are plugged into computers to record changes in the magnetic field when the investigator is absent.

Such equipment can take up a lot of room, as Peter Underwood writes in *Ghosts and How to See Them:* "I knew one . . . hunter who took over five tons of equipment with him, and another who had a van permanently loaded with every type of [poltergeist-hunting] equipment you can imagine."[40]

Whether or not such tools really measure the presence of ghosts remains unknown. Those who are unconvinced point out that a person sufficiently determined to see a poltergeist might, in good faith, interpret the findings of gadgets as proving the existence of something that is not there.

While information generated by EMF meters is open to interpretation, some poltergeist hunters have taken courses on forensics, the scientific techniques used by police to collect minute clues at crime scenes that can be used as evidence. This training allows investigators to record fingerprints and analyze blood and other stains that may indicate a human presence at the alleged site of a poltergeist disturbance.

Those practicing forensic hypnotism can hypnotize witnesses or others present at a disturbance and access their deep, repressed memories of an event. Hypnotism also may help a subject remember foggy or forgotten details of a case.

Some investigators go beyond forensics and have college degrees in psychology so they can better determine the credibility—and mental stability—of witnesses. As John Cutten, secretary of the SPR, says: "Often what we are really doing is investigating the person rather than what they claim to see or experience." [41]

Extensive Interviews

Dedicated poltergeist hunters face several problems that may hinder their investigations. Unlike ghostly hauntings that may take place over extended periods of time, poltergeist hauntings are usually short in duration. This fact has prompted Roll to write: "If intensive research is to be undertaken, the investigator must arrive at the scene as soon as possible." [42] In recent decades, investigators may also find that the media has been notified and the haunted site is crowded with reporters and camera operators. In such cases researchers must negotiate with the press to postpone publicity and the resultant throngs of people that can hinder scientific inquiry into the haunting, as Underwood writes:

> Families are often highly embarrassed and even frightened by newspaper, radio and television reporters.

A parapsychologist questions Jimmy Herrmann to learn if he is responsible for the poltergeist disturbances in his family's household.

There have been many instances where thoughtless words have brought hordes of people to a reportedly haunted house and eventually, in an effort to stop the unwelcome attention, the occupants have said that nothing really happened and they were mistaken all the time. [43]

During a poltergeist investigation in Brazil, a researcher (right) interviews a witness immediately after the disturbance to gather accurate information.

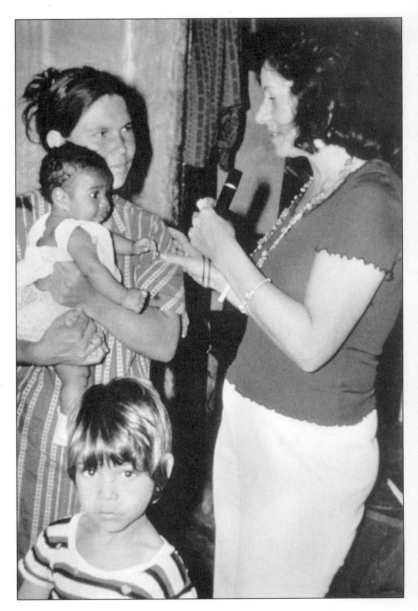

Before an investigator does "field work" examining evidence, he or she must conduct extensive interviews with witnesses, family members, and others who may have been involved. Each person is interviewed separately and asked to describe exactly what was seen, heard, felt, and even smelled. They are asked to describe what they think happened, what their theory is as to the cause of the disturbance. This is done because if someone thinks that their house is definitely haunted, they may unknowingly misreport their experiences to back up this belief. Or if they are extremely religious, they may perceive a satanic force when a poltergeist might be to blame. At the other end of the belief spectrum, those who refuse to believe in poltergeist phenomena may firmly believe that a prowler or mischievous child is at fault. While conducting interviews, investigators never forget that someone might be perpetrating a fraud or hoax, as Underwood writes:

> Tony Cornell, president of the Cambridge University Society for Psychical Research, once told me about a case that he looked into where a widower lived alone, the rest of the family having fled from the house "because of a poltergeist." After talking to the old man for some time—interrupted by the occasional "bump" and "bang" that seemed to have no cause or reason— Tony noticed that just prior to any of the noises the old fellow was quietly pulling on a piece of wire. He had rigged up his own ghost! It transpired that he had felt he was not wanted by his family, so he had driven them all out of the house. [44]

Just the Facts

To sort out often conflicting stories—and to save precious time—some psychic investigators use detailed questionnaires for eyewitnesses. They may ask standard questions such as location and duration of the disturbance. More detailed questions surround birthdays, anniversaries, or other significant dates. A day that is of importance to a witness may indicate that he or she is involved with the event.

The behavior of pets is often a clue, as dogs, cats, and birds sometimes behave strangely when a disturbance is taking place. Farm animals, especially horses, are said to be particularly sensitive to the presence of spirits, and have been known to whinny and stomp their feet when alleged poltergeists are nearby.

Most important, researchers need to know if any pubescent or adolescent children live in the house as they are often the focus of poltergeist activity. Interviewers should also take special care when talking to those who have an interest in paranormal phenomena, as Roll writes:

> If the persons involved have had psychic experiences in the past, particularly if they are similar to the present occurrences, this may indicate that the persons are important for the phenomena, perhaps as ESP percipients of ghosts, or PK agents of poltergeist disturbances. Sometimes a description of supposed previous psychical experiences indicates that these are only the effects of an imaginative or diseased mind and that perhaps the present phenomena can be explained in the same way. If the persons have been excessively interested in psychic or occult matters in the past, it may be possible that the present incidents are only due to imagination or exaggeration of ordinary happenings. [45]

Physical Evidence

During interviews, investigators take careful notes as to the exact time and place of disturbances. This information may be charted on a floorplan of the house to determine if the events were in the presence of a specific family member or occurred in empty rooms near a human agent. After determining that the disturbance is not the work of a misguided individual or charlatan hoping to create publicity, the site of the haunting must be painstakingly investigated. This often involves site preparation in which all doors and windows are shut tight so that temperature drops or slammed doors cannot be attributed to the wind. In some cases pieces of thread or tape are laid across window sills so that if a window is opened and closed, inves-

Advice for Poltergeist Victims

When someone's home becomes the focus of a poltergeist disturbance, few victims know where to turn. In *This House Is Haunted,* renowned psychic investigator Guy Playfair offers some words of advice to those who believe they are suffering from a poltergeist:

The first thing to do if a poltergeist invades [a] home is to identify the epicenter person. In many cases, but not all, this will be a boy or girl near the age of puberty, and as an emergency measure the epicenter should be separated from the rest of the family. This will probably not solve the problem permanent-ly, but at least it will enable the rest of the family to get some sleep. . . .

Perhaps the most important thing to do when poltergeist activity breaks out is not to panic. Nothing truly awful is likely to happen, and it is most unlikely that [the family's] little girl is possessed by demons, which the popular press may well suggest if given the chance. It will help if [the family tries] to take an objective interest in what is going on, noting incidents as they happen, and if possible photographing them and making tape recordings.

tigators will see that it has been disturbed. In drastic cases, where pranksters might be suspected of tricking investigators, windows and doors may be nailed shut so that there is absolutely no chance that they could be opened.

Once a site is secured, investigators might patrol every room in the house every fifteen to thirty minutes. This is done to determine if doors are opened, lights are turned off or on, or furniture has been moved. Between patrols, investigators sit in the dark and remain perfectly silent. Any unusual sounds or movements are recorded in a notebook, along with weather phenomena such as wind, rain, and snow. In order to fight off sleep, investigators may stroll around the grounds to peer into rooms from the outside through the windows.

However, as all investigators understand, poltergeists do not appear on demand. Many investigators have spent long hours sitting in the dark, waiting for a paranormal disturbance. As widely read psychic investigator Hans Holzer writes in *Ghost Hunter,* poltergeists "do not perform like trained circus animals, just to please a group of skeptics or sensation seekers. Then too, one should remember that . . . [a] sympathetic visitor would encourage [a poltergeist]; a hostile onlooker inhibit it."[46]

When a Poltergeist Appears

Oftentimes investigators will never actually see objects thrown, furniture moved, fires spontaneously ignited, and so on. In such cases, the investigator can still work with the victims to determine the possible causes of their problems. This may involve counseling a disturbed teenager who is emitting PK energy or recommending that an exorcism or séance be conducted to drive out the poltergeist.

Maurice Grosse and Guy Playfair, psychic investigators in the Janet Harper poltergeist case, study disturbed furniture as Janet watches from her bed.

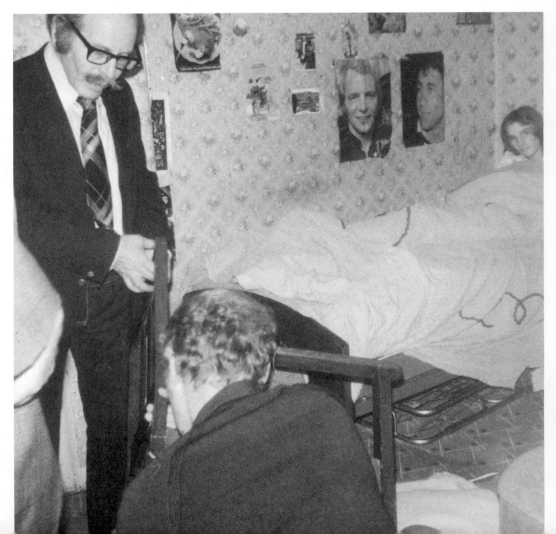

In some cases where there is extremely strong or repetitive poltergeist commotion, psychic investigators actually witness disturbances, often for weeks on end. When Playfair investigated the extreme poltergeist activity surrounding Janet Harper, an eleven-year-old girl in Enfield, England, he saw so much activity that "the case was turning into a monotonous routine, with the same incidents happening over and over again—beds shaking, marbles and Legos flying about, drawers opening and chairs falling over."[47]

In such cases, investigators write up reports and immediately draw diagrams. The trajectory of a moving object is mapped and a sketch is drawn demonstrating its path across a room or from a table to the floor. The weight of the object is noted along with other miscellaneous observations. As always, trickery should be promptly investigated; as Underwood writes, investigators should explore "the possibility that a thread or wire could have been loosely attached to the object, or that it could have been projected some other way by normal means. [Researchers should search] carefully for any signs of cotton, paste, chewing gum or anything similar that might hold an object for a limited time."[48]

As another method of preventing deception, investigators try to keep track of everyone in the house. When disturbances occur, the researcher will want to know who was near the alleged incident and what others were doing when it occurred.

The best reward for any investigator is to capture a poltergeist disturbance on film. Photos or videos can be studied for hours by investigators trying to piece together details of an incident. Photographing poltergeists can be rather tricky, however, as Underwood writes:

While the question of whether or not [poltergeists] can be photographed is still open to question, there are a number of photographs that seem to be genuine and appear to depict a form or figure that may or may not be seen by the photographer. So it is always worth taking photographs whenever the temperature drops; whenever anyone has the feeling that something is about to happen . . . or, indeed, whenever . . . it might be worth taking a photo. You never know, something may appear on film.[49]

Photos can also detect trickery. Photographers have actually caught people staging fake poltergeist disturbances, stealthily throwing objects. And while genuine photographs may be used to convince a skeptical public, film and digital photos can also be easily adulterated. Charlatans have been caught doctoring photos to look as if objects were moved by an invisible hand.

Paradoxes and Problems

Fake photos, invisible wires, and other methods for committing poltergeist fraud are just some of the problems faced by psychic investigators. Perhaps the hardest to overcome is the basic paradox of poltergeist investigation. While a hunter has to be constantly on the lookout for deception, he or she must also believe in the existence of poltergeists, ghosts, and other paranormal activity. The suspension of disbelief must often take place in the face of intense public scrutiny and skepticism, forcing the poltergeist hunter to question constantly his or her beliefs. Underwood answers this dilemma by stating:

> It should be realized and accepted that there is nothing credulous or gullible about someone investigating haunted houses and similar phenomena. Either such phenomena do occur, or they do not, and either way it is the task of the psychic investigator to study and record such happenings, or lack of them, in a perfectly calm, cool and judicial manner.[50]

While this may be possible, hunting for poltergeists is not a job for the thin-skinned or easily defeated. Few understand this better than psychic researcher J.B. Rhine who pioneered research into PK phenomena and poltergeist hauntings. When

Psychic investigator J.B. Rhine conducted groundbreaking research into the connection between PK phenomena and poltergeist activity.

confronting the problems faced by poltergeist hunters, Rhine asks why anyone would want to take on such a job:

> Why on earth does anyone do research on poltergeists? It is easy enough for most of us to be interested in these very odd and annoying disruptions of the household, if only out of sympathy for the families that suffer them, but it is quite another matter to be willing to invest what it takes in the patient effort, limitless inconvenience, embarrassing publicity, disturbed sleep, and tireless energy that are demanded in actual investigation.[51]

The answers to these questions may be as elusive as the poltergeists themselves. However, as long as there are mysterious noises that go bump in the night, there will be people who will stop at nothing to find answers to the baffling questions posed by purported poltergeist activity.

Chapter 4

Poltergeist Communications

Whenstimes, however, the spirits are said to communicate with words that might be in an
unknown language or simply in gibberish. Whatever the case,When poltergeists commit their mischief, the pandemonium is purportedly accompanied by rapping, screeching, popping, and other thunderous noises. It is also said that poltergeists may sometimes attempt to communicate to witnesses messages that are delivered, according to Bayless, in "[yells], screams, bellows, whistlings, whispers, laughs, sobs, grunts, and every imaginable sound possible."[52]

In past centuries it was the rare poltergeist event that did not include a report of some sort of message delivered by the spirit. These were alleged to materialize from thin air or blast through a range of items including vases, flowers, and trumpets. Communication might be through a single word, a threatening sentence, a song, or endless paragraphs filled with bizarre lectures.

Some messages delivered by poltergeists have been clear and needed no interpretation. Oftentimes, however, the spirits are said to communicate with words that might be in an unknown language or simply in gibberish. Whatever the case, poltergeist voices seem to develop and change during the course of a haunting, according to Colin Wilson in *Poltergeist!: A Study in Destructive Haunting:*

> Poltergeist voices . . . do not sound like ordinary human voices; at least not to begin with. It seems as if the entity is having to master a strange medium, to

form sounds into words. (Even the rapping noises are probably "manufactured" sounds, not genuine raps) made by hard objects. Most talking . . . poltergeists begin in a guttural voice that sounds as if it is made up from grunts and groans; [in one case the spirit] made gasping, whispering noises more like an asthmatic cough. Gradually the voice developed until it was a low audible whisper. . . . [The voice] graduated from a whisper to a normal voice. . . . Then it began to use bad language—again a common characteristic of talking [poltergeists].[53]

In some cases, mediums are summoned in order to interpret the words of the poltergeist, and possibly reply to the spirit's message. Mediums are so-called because they work between the earthly world and the world of spirits. To communicate with poltergeists, a medium voluntarily "channels" the spirit in order to allow it to possess his or her body. The poltergeist may then express its desires through the medium by speech or through a process called automatic writing in

Counting Fingers

It is often reported that poltergeists have the ability to communicate by making knocking noises. In a nineteenth-century case in Ireland, farmer Thomas Plunkett tested a poltergeist's counting abilities—and assured himself that the knocking could not be the work of pranksters. Plunkett's description of the event is printed in *Poltergeists* by Sacheverell Sitwell:

I mentally asked [the poltergeist], no word being spoken, to knock a certain number of times and it did so. To avoid any error or delusion on my part, I put my hands in the side pockets of my overcoat and asked it to knock the number of fingers I had open. It correctly did so. Then, with a different number of fingers open each time, the experiment was repeated four times in succession, and four times I obtained absolutely the correct number of raps. The doctrine of chances shows that casual coincidence is here practically out of the question, and the interesting fact remains that some telepathic rapport between the unseen agent and ourselves appears to exist, on this occasion at any rate.

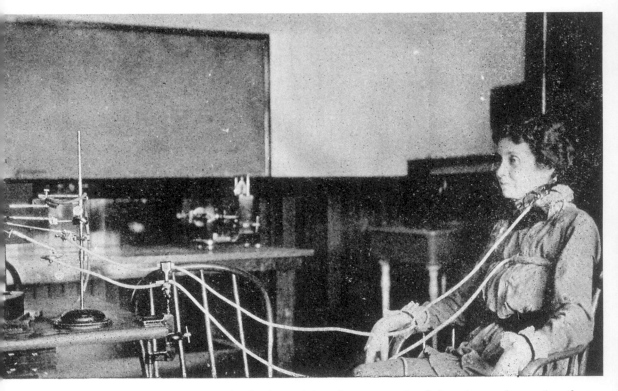

In this 1914 photograph, a medium is hooked up to a kymograph, a machine designed to distinguish ghostly voices from the medium's own voice.

which the spirit takes control of the channeler to jot down words or pictures. Of course, throughout history, some dishonest mediums have been expert ventriloquists; that is they could speak without perceptible movement of the lips, "throwing" their voices so that the sounds seem to emanate from a different room. For those unfamiliar with ventriloquism, the effects could be startling.

Mocking Words

Whether or not ventriloquism played any role in some of the oldest records of poltergeist communications is unknown. However, these ancient incidents were believed to have come directly from a spirit, with no mediums involved. Although they happened in different centuries, and hundreds of miles apart, the cases seem to be eerily similar. The oldest record of poltergeist communication comes from Kembden, a village on the Rhine River in present-day Germany. In A.D. 858, peasants were allegedly abused by a poltergeist that created cacophonous noises and reined stones down on their houses. A human voice was said to come out of the sky, mocking the witnesses and loudly relating details of their most intimate activities. One villager in particular was singled out for carrying on a clandestine love affair. His possessions were consequently destroyed in a mysterious fire, and this ended the communications.

More than three hundred years after the mysterious Kembden poltergeist incident, residents of the English town of Pembrokeshire reported another talkative spirit. In 1184, this entity threw dirt and stones, and ripped apart or made holes in linens and clothing. The poltergeist was said to expose the deeds of the village men who tried to talk to it, according to an account written by author Giraldus Cambrensis around 1191:

> [The] spirit used to talk with men, and when people bandied words with it, as many did in mockery, it taxed them with all the things they had ever done in their lives which they were least willing should be known or spoken about. [54]

It is unclear how or why a poltergeist would know about the deepest secrets held by the townsmen. Such activity, however, seems to fit the pattern of rude, mischievous spirits often associated with poltergeist cases.

If these reports were true, the speech may have come from one of two sources. According to psychic researchers, the words were either delivered by a genuine spirit with the intelligence and free will to speak its mind, or the words were "projected" through PK energy by a human agent responsible for the poltergeist activities. This human agent might have overheard people discussing their private lives or simply mentioned private acts usually done behind closed doors that could have been common to any of the villagers.

A Clairvoyant Maid?

In theory, someone who can utilize PK energy may also be telepathic or clairvoyant. That is, they can perceive things beyond the natural range of the senses. This might have been the situation of the often amusing poltergeist said to haunt a home in Geneva, Switzerland, in 1644.

The Geneva poltergeist allegedly whistled a well-known tune called "Minister, Minister" between whistles that were shrill and painful to the ears of those present. Soon the spirit was willing to speak to witnesses, reciting garbled religious prayers and offering to transform itself into an angel of light. Abandoning its religious façade, the poltergeist sang a lewd song called "Le Filou" ("The Rascal") complete with dirty words and obscene verses. The spirit was also adept at mimicking the voices of local jugglers and huntsmen. On a humorous note, it informed a gathering in a pained and moaning voice that it was on its deathbed and that the housemaid should go get a lawyer so it could make its will.

The vocalizations of this poltergeist may have been traceable to the maid who was the only person who seemed to be unafraid of the impudent spirit. During séances, the poltergeist spoke intimately with the maid, and some of the observers believed the woman was a witch. On one occasion, she demanded that the spirit provide her with firewood, and a pile of logs allegedly was thrown down from the ceiling. When the girl was replaced with another maid, the substitute was driven away after being beaten and soaked with water, purportedly by the poltergeist. While the haunting was traced to the maid, the poltergeist spoke with an accent unknown to the maid and the spirit was able to mimic people the maid had never met. Owen hypothesizes that the maid might have had multiple personality disorder and had a separate personality that she seemed unaware of, and that she was able to psychically learn the voices of the jugglers and huntsmen she imitated:

If we assume that the speech was ventriloquism, the only really likely candidate as ventriloquist would be the maid. The difference in accent would be difficult to achieve. It remains very remarkable in relation to the "unconscious personality" theory of the poltergeist as applied to the maid. . . . [We] find that the demon was indeed a remarkable mimic, counterfeiting voices of people present *and* of people "he" had not "met." If [people accept] the truth of the narrative, then it may be agreed that this mimicry suggests telepathic or clairvoyant awareness [in the maid] in the speech forms of various persons.[55]

Torments of the Bell Witch

Many times, poltergeist voices can be harsh and nasty, and may sound as if they are coming from more than one spirit. In such cases, the poltergeist may be imitating several different "people," or it may be a multiple haunting. In 1817, the John Bell family of Robertson County, Tennessee, was visited by what seemed to be a family of poltergeists.

There were nine children in the Bell household, and several of them were adolescents or teenagers. The event began

A teenage boy surveys his bedroom after an alleged occurrence of poltergeist activity. Adolescents are typically at the center of such activity.

as many do, with slightly strange sounds, as if rats were gnawing inside the walls. As the noises intensified, the family heard an invisible dog scratching the floor, an invisible bird flapping around the room, and two other dogs that sounded as if they were fighting. Choking and gulping sounds accompanied other phenomena, such as flying objects, cloddings, and severe hair pulling reported by family members.

The focus of this activity seemed to be Betsy, Bell's twelve-year-old daughter. Events grew worse until the family was utterly distraught. John Bell's tongue swelled to double its size, and he felt as if someone was pushing a stick into his mouth. Then the spirit, now known by the neighbors as the "Bell Witch," allegedly began to talk. At first it said, "I am a spirit who was once very happy, but have been disturbed and am now unhappy." [56] Soon the spirit claimed it was different characters, including a Native American who was once buried on the site and a witch called Old Kate Batts. Four more voices were later heard from the Bell Witch: Blackdog spoke in a gruff male voice, often sounding drunk and allegedly filling the house with the smell of whiskey when he visited; Jerusalem spoke as a young boy; and creatures identifying themselves as Mathematics and Cypocryphy were frail and feminine.

While the witch promised to torment John Bell for the rest of his life, it was much kinder to family members. When John's wife, Lucy, was ill, hazelnuts are said to have rained on her sickbed. On Betsy's birthday it announced that it had a surprise for her from the West Indies and delivered a basket of oranges and bananas, fruit that was not available in Tennessee at that time.

A local doctor realized Betsy was the focus and gave her a vile medicine that made her vomit up brass pins and needles. The voice laughed and said if the doctor gave the girl more of the medicine, she would have enough pins to start her own sewing shop.

Finally, the Bell Witch tormented John Bell with shrieks, curses, derision, and physical beatings that were so terrible the man could barely leave his bed. In 1820, three years after the attacks began, Bell took an overdose of medicine that killed him. When the Bell Witch found out, it allegedly filled the house with joyous caterwauling and sang a song called "Row Me Up Some Brandy, O." After several months of peace, the Bell Witch returned and said, "I am going, and will be gone for seven years—goodbye to all." [57] As promised, poltergeist activities started again seven years later, but they were mild and quickly ceased.

The case of the Bell Witch attracted quite a bit of attention when John Bell's son Robert wrote a book about the events in 1846. In later years, various researchers have tried to explain the case. Psychiatrist Nandor Fodor put forth the theory that Betsy was the victim of incest by her father and the young girl repeatedly expressed her repressed hatred in the form of PK energy. This was done, Fodor believes, when a fragment of personality separated from the girl and was able to speak and create havoc. Owen offers his own hypothesis on the Bell haunting:

> [It] was the work of a group of rowdy and mischievous spirits or "elementals" of no particular intelligence—the other-worldly equivalent of a cageful of monkeys. A house with nine children, many of them teenagers, would provide plenty of energy poltergeists find necessary to perform their antics. . . . No doubt John Bell was a typical nineteenth-century patriarch, dictatorial and bad-tempered; and on a farmstead in a remote rural area, there was no doubt plenty of reason for tension and frustration in the family. [58]

Ultimately, the existence of the Bell Witch remains in question. Some psychic researchers theorize that Robert Bell may have invented the poltergeist solely to write his book.

The Message and the Medium

While it is often alleged that poltergeists are speaking to victims of hauntings, it is less common for a poltergeist to communicate through the written word. Nonetheless, that is exactly what was alleged during the poltergeist incidents at Borley Rectory. In 1930 when Reverend Lionel Foyster moved into the rectory with his wife, Marianne, the Foysters found themselves mysteriously locked out of rooms while household items began to disappear. On some nights, while the couple cow-

The Writing on the Wall

In the early 1930s, mysterious written words began to appear on the walls of Borley Rectory in England, apparently addressed to resident Marianne Foyster. While psychic investigator Harry Price questioned whether an incarnate spirit can sharpen a pencil, he nonetheless believed the words were created by a poltergeist. Price described the seemingly meaningless messages in *The Most Haunted House in England*:

> The first writing, "Marianne," was found on the wall by the stairs leading to the bathroom passage. . . . The next message we found was on the outside wall of the bathroom . . . and reads: "Marianne At Get Help—Entant Bottom Me". . . . It is partly meaningless, and one word suggests "repentant." Underneath the message is printed in capitals "I cannot understand, tell me more." Those words were written by Mrs. Foyster, hoping that a second "message" would elucidate the first. . . . The answering

message . . . was almost undecipherable, but the following words or letters can be made out: "Light in **** Write Prayer and O ****". . . . The last, and most interesting message, was found on the landing archway. . . . It read: "Get Light Mass and Prayer Here."

In the 1930s, messages to Marianne Foyster were scrawled on the walls of Borley Rectory in England, where Foyster lived.

ered in their bed, windows shattered, furniture was loudly dragged from room to room, and loud rapping from inside the walls echoed through the house. The most frightening incidents, however, involved Marianne Foyster, as Troy Taylor describes on the "Borley Rectory: The History of 'The Most Haunted House in England'" Web site:

> [Marianne Foyster] was thrown from her bed at night, slapped by invisible hands, forced to dodge heavy objects which flew at her day and night, and was once almost suffocated with a mattress. Soon after, there began to appear a series of scrawled messages on the walls of the house, written by an unknown hand. They seemed to be pleading with Mrs. Foyster, using phrases like "Marianne, please help" . . . and "Marianne light mass prayers."[59]

Understandably the Foysters left Borley Rectory in 1933. In 1937, ghost hunter Price rented the abandoned house for a year and moved in with a team of ghost hunters

Destroyed by fire in 1939, Borley Rectory is still famous as the site of the most intense poltergeist activity ever investigated.

who worked around the clock in order to document any manifestations of spirits. The bizarre poltergeist activity continued unabated and included appearances of puddles of brown water and glue-like substances, along with foul odors similar to a backed up toilet. Despite the evidence, the investigators were unable to determine the source of the hauntings until another method of communication was employed.

Remains Buried in Cellar

Between October 23 and 25, 1937, Price and several others met with a medium named Sidney H. Glanville to conduct a series of séances at the rectory. These were conducted with several people sitting around a table. In the center, they had a device known as a planchette, described by Price as "a heart-shaped piece of wood at the apex of which a sharpened lead pencil is inserted. . . . At the other end of the [planchette] are two small . . . wheels or castors in order that it can be made to move easily over a sheet of paper when hands are rested on it."[60]

While four people each put a hand on the planchette, it spelled out a story allegedly dictated by a spirit named Marie Lairre. Responses to a series of mostly yes-or-no questions indicated that the phantasm had died in the seventeenth century. A French nun, she had left her convent to marry a Henry Waldegrave, a member of a wealthy family whose manor home had once stood on the site of the rectory. The marriage was short and unhappy, ending when Waldegrave strangled Lairre and buried her remains in the cellar. Lairre told the assembled ghost hunters that she wished her bones to be buried in a proper cemetery after a requiem mass celebrated by a Catholic priest.

Price believed that this story was corroborated by the messages that the apparition had written about a mass and prayers to Marianne Foyster. He concluded that unless her request was fulfilled, the poltergeist of the nun would haunt the rectory forever.

Five months later, in March 1938, the ghost hunters held another session with the planchette, this time in a nearby town. At this séance a different spirit appeared, this one apparently a fire-starting poltergeist. Calling himself Sunex Amures, he told the ghost hunters in clipped language: "MEAN TO BURN THE RECTORY to-night at 9 o'clock end of the haunting go to the rectory and you will be able to . . . find bone of murdered [nun] under the ruins . . . you will have proof of haunting of the rectory at Borley . . . [which] tells the story of murder which happened there."[61]

Nothing happened that night, or the next, but exactly eleven months later after a new tenant, Captain W.H. Gregson, moved in, Borley Rectory burned to the ground. That night while unpacking some books, Gregson accidentally knocked over an oil lamp and the fire quickly gutted the rectory, leaving only the brick outer walls standing.

Possibly because his work was interrupted by World War II, Price did not attempt to find the remains of Marie Lairre until 1943, at which time he found several fragile human bones under the brick floor in the cellar. They were given a proper burial, and no further hauntings were reported at the ruins of the rectory, which was finally demolished by townspeople in 1944. In this case it seems that several spirits communicated messages meant to help investigators find answers to the poltergeist activity.

Skeptics do not accept such theories, however. Some point to the fact that in later years Marianne Foyster admitted that the writings traced to a poltergeist only seemed to occur when Edwin Whitehouse, the nephew of the rectory's overseer, was present. Whitehouse was mentally disturbed from his experiences in World War I. After he

The Mind Moving Matter

In the case of the Borley Rectory, communication was conducted with poltergeists through a planchette, a writing device that spelled out answers as séance participants rested their hands upon it. According to Robert Todd Carroll on "The Skeptic's Dictionary" Web site, such devices are unconsciously moved by participants, not poltergeists, through what is called the ideomotor effect:

> The ideomotor effect refers to the influence of suggestion on involuntary and unconscious motor behavior. The term "ideomotor action" was coined by William B. Carpenter in 1852 in his explanation for the movements of . . . some table turning or lifting by spirit mediums (the ones that weren't accomplished by cheating). Carpenter argued that muscular movement can be initiated by the mind independently of volition or emotions. We may not be aware of it, but suggestions can be made to the mind by others or by observations. Those suggestions can influence the mind and affect motor behavior.

Skeptics maintain that unconscious motor behavior is responsible for the movement of the planchette across the Ouija board.

stopped visiting, the writing stopped. As to the messages from the planchette sessions, skeptics say that in such cases the writing implement can be moved either consciously or unconsciously by those attending the séance. Unnoticeable movements by the medium, not paranormal forces, moved the planchette.

Utter and Complete Fraud?

While it might be easy to dismiss the activity at Borley, it occurred over an extended period of time while dozens of witnesses were in the house. And it seemed to some to have a sensible cause and conclusion. In most cases, however, alleged hauntings are short and often inconclusive. For example, in a seventeenth-century case in Newbury, England, purported poltergeists tormented a family for only several weeks. When the end of the disturbance was near, the troublesome spirits allegedly said, "We knock and demonstrate no more."[62] To some, this may sound like an announcement from a badly behaved neighbor announcing that he is done playing a practical joke on the family. And oftentimes, poltergeist communications have such sources. Many emanate from deceitful mediums practicing ventriloquism and naive witnesses who take such experiences at face value. As Bayless writes:

> I have sat hour upon hour listening to these vocal marvels—all the product of utter and complete fraud! . . . At times, I have been amused, but usually bored, and on numerous occasions revolted and disgusted. The appalling thing is not the fraud and duplicity of the medium (that can be expected), or the ruthless, callous greed that is so many times displayed, but the gullibility of the spectators and believers.

> It seems that no matter how inconceivably crude or childish the fakery may be, there are always followers

who are willing to swallow the ridiculous performances whole. One would think that the very content of the messages alone would give rise to suspicion, but no matter how foolish the speech, the medium's circle is always eager and happy to accept all without the slightest doubt. [63]

Despite his exposure of fraud, Bayless believes in poltergeists. So while the message and the medium may be fake, many still say that something is out there creating these disturbances. Whether human or spirit, incarnate or disincarnate, no one can say for sure.

Chapter 5

When Poltergeists Attack

A s annoying and frightening as poltergeists can be, victims of hauntings are seldom injured. In the majority of cases, poltergeists create their mischief and move on, leaving witnesses and researchers with dozens of questions and few answers. History is filled, however, with cases of poltergeists that bite, wound, scar, and even kill their victims. For reasons that defy explanation, these hostile spirits take great joy in tormenting until the victims are driven to insanity or death.

Compared to the overall number of poltergeist disturbances, those that involve assault are relatively uncommon. But as Gauld and Cornell write: "Uncommon, perhaps, but not unknown. . . . Sometimes poltergeists have been wildly, one might say insanely, violent and destructive."[64] Stories about these vicious spirits have been told for thousands of years.

Spirits That Bite

The least harmful of physical attacks said to have been perpetrated by poltergeists appear in the form of animal-like bites that can appear anywhere on a victim's body. One of the most well-known attacks was described in a pamphlet written by Henry Durbin called "A Narrative of Some Extraordinary

There are cases of alleged poltergeist attacks on people that leave marks resembling animal bites or scratches on the victim's body.

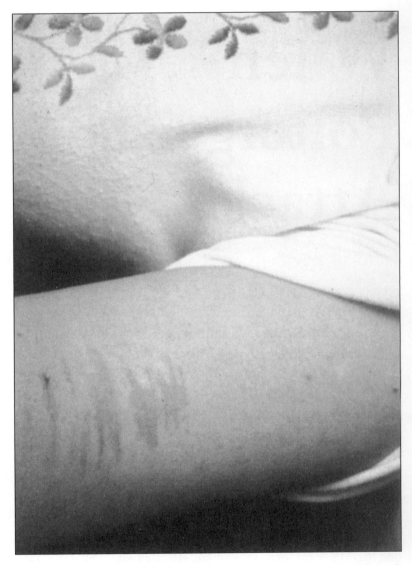

Things That Happened to Mr. Richard Giles's Children." The Giles children, Molly and Dobby, two adolescent girls in Bristol, England, were tormented by a violent poltergeist. Although Durbin originally investigated the case in order to debunk it, he was quickly convinced that a malicious spirit was at work.

The torments began in December 1761, when objects such as wine glasses began flying about the Giles house without reason. When the activity increased, a local admiral and other respected townsmen, including Durbin, moved into the house in order to witness the phenomena and attempt to find a cure. On February 19, Molly and Dobby were dragged from their beds by an unseen force. When three men tried to hold on to them, a tug-of-war ensued with the children shrieking in the middle. The men, however, were no match for the invisible force, and the children were cruelly thrown around their bedroom.

Events increased in intensity as an invisible hand allegedly tried to strangle Molly as Durbin watched helplessly. As the astonished witness wrote, "I saw the flesh at the side of her throat pushed in, whiten as if done with fingers, though I saw none. Her face grew red and blackish presently, as if she was strangled, but without any convulsion."[65] In the days that followed, Molly was cut forty times by an unseen agent. Both

Traction

When poltergeists violently pull or push victims, the phenomenon is called traction of the human body. A well-known case of traction was first recorded by Henry Durbin in 1800 concerning two adolescent sisters, Molly and Dobby Giles. Durbin's description is found in *Can We Explain the Poltergeist?* by A.R.G. Owen:

The children had been pulled out of bed several times . . . by the neck, in [the full view of three men]. The children lay on their back, and I saw very strong gentlemen hold each child under their arms as they lay on their back: they soon cried out they were pulled by the legs. [One of the men] Major D—held Molly with all his might, and put his knee against her bedstead, but cried he could not hold her, the force was so great that he thought three [hundred pounds] pulled against him. They were both pulled to the foot of the bed and the Major fell on the bed. . . . I saw the children as often pulled to the bed's foot, and both the Major and the other gentlemen pulled after them, though they held them with all their strength, the children crying with pain. They felt hands pull them by their legs, and I saw black and blue marks on the small of their legs, as if hands had done it. I held Dobby myself, under the arms . . . but I found my strength nothing to the force which pulled against me, and she was pulled to the bed's foot and then it stopped.

children experienced pinching that was so powerful there were marks from fingernails left in the flesh. Although Durbin compared the wounds to those of the children and others in the room, they did not match the nails of anyone present. Then the biting began, as Durbin writes:

> [Seven] of us being there in the room . . . Molly said she was bit in the arm, and presently Dobby cried out the same. We saw their arms bitten about twenty times that evening. Their arms were put out of bed, and they lay on their backs. They could not do it themselves, as we were looking at them the whole time. We examined the bites and found on them the impression of eighteen or twenty teeth, with saliva or spittle all over them in the shape of a mouth, almost all of them very wet, and the spittle [steaming in the cold], as if just spit out of the mouth. I took up some of it on my finger to try the consistency of it, and [another witness] did the same, and we found it clammy like spittle, and it smelt rank. [66]

This event left about a teacupful of spittle on the girls; spit also allegedly dripped from the ceiling, although no source of the disturbance was ever found.

In more recent years, poltergeist researcher Roll reported seeing "mysterious bat-like bites" [67] on Renate Beck, Linda Beck, thirteen, and Renate's mother, Lina Gemmecke. The victims lived in Indianapolis, and the bites were first incurred by Renate in March 1962 after she heard a vase fall from a shelf. As she investigated, she received five nasty puncture wounds above her right wrist. A few days later, Renate and Gemmecke were sitting in the kitchen when they were attacked by invisible biting creatures that left marks similar to those left by bat fangs. The victims were tormented for weeks as they were bitten in twenty-nine separate incidents on their arms, necks, breasts, thighs, and elsewhere. Sometimes blood flowed from the wounds, and the skin around the bites was discolored for weeks after the punctures disappeared. Linda,

In the early 1960s, parapsychologist William Roll investigated the violent poltergeist attacks against Lina Gemmecke and her daughter that left batlike bites on their bodies.

however, never received a single bite and took little interest in the horror visited upon her mother and grandmother.

The bites stopped when a new series of phenomena ensued, including flying objects and intense rapping and knocking. Police were called on one particularly violent day, and Gemmecke was crazed with fear. When a detective approached, Gemmecke, in her agitated state, might have believed the officer was a poltergeist. The elderly woman screamed, threw an ashtray at him, and overturned several pieces of furniture. Police arrested

Gemmecke for disturbing the peace and took her to jail. As far as the detective was concerned, the case was solved, as Roll writes:

> It seemed clear to him that here was the instigator of all the disturbances, which had brought several investigations and visits by members of his department. He arrested Mrs. Gemmecke on a charge of disorderly conduct.
>
> As far as the police and newspapers were concerned, the case of the strange "bat bites," knockings, and movements of objects had been solved and the culprit had been clearly identified as Mrs. Gemmecke. [68]

Authorities and the media failed to explain, however, how the woman was able to bite herself on the back of the neck and other unreachable places.

After she was released on bail the next day, Gemmecke was convinced that both the poltergeist and the police were out to get her. She soon moved out of her daughter's house and returned to her native Germany. Departing from his usual theory that the teenager is often the PK agent in poltergeist hauntings, Roll believes that Renate Beck was the cause of the problem, focusing intense hostility on her mother. For complex psychological reasons, Gemmecke played the role of a secondary agent unconsciously helping her daughter create the misery. Whatever the case, the violence of the biting, bleeding, and bruising divided the family and succeeded in driving an elderly woman from the home.

A Persistently Malevolent Poltergeist

Whatever the source of the Indiana attacks, it seems as if the poltergeist forces were trying to accomplish a specific mission—driving Gemmecke from the house. The disturbances ceased after the woman left. Three years later in Jabuticabal, Brazil, 220 miles from São Paulo, a purported poltergeist had no such clear-cut mission. To observers, it seemed as if this demonic force was simply taking joy in the torments—and eventual murder—of a young girl.

Problems began in December 1965, when pieces of brick began falling from the ceiling in the home of an unnamed family. A priest was called who attempted an exorcism, which instantly made things much worse. This caused the family to contact their neighbor Joáo Volpe, a dentist, who had studied the work of the spiritualist Kardec. Volpe noticed that the focus of the disturbance was the eleven-year-old Maria José Ferreira, daughter of a housemaid who slept in the servant's quarters.

The dentist felt that Ferreira was a natural medium who was unconsciously allowing the poltergeist activity to take place. Volpe took the girl into his home for observation. After a few days, stones began flying around the house until Volpe was able to count 312 stones, including one that weighed nearly nine pounds. On one occasion when the family was dining, a large stone fell from the ceiling and split in two in midair, with each piece flying in a different direction. When they were picked up by a witness, the stones snapped together as if they were magnetic.

Meanwhile, Ferreira seemed to make friends with her invisible hosts. If she voiced the desire for a flower, jewelry, or a piece of candy, the requested items would allegedly appear at her feet. These happy events did not last long, however. Although poltergeist stone-throwing incidents rarely harm their targets, for unknown reasons the stone attacks became

A poltergeist tormented the eleven-year-old Maria José Ferreira of Brazil with violent showers of stones and rocks like these.

more violent, shattering glass tabletops and falling on Ferreira's plates during meals. This event was followed by a three-week nonstop attack in which every piece of crockery, dinnerware, and other breakable items was destroyed within the Volpe household.

The spirit soon increased its hostilities, prompting Guy Playfair to define it in *Indefinite Boundary* as "one of the most persistently malevolent poltergeists in history."[69] With invisible hands and teeth the force began to pinch, slap, and bite Ferreira. Witnesses say they saw this malicious poltergeist throw chairs, pictures, mirrors, and even a large sofa at the girl. Not content to torture her with these horrors, the poltergeist allegedly tried to kill Ferreira. Cups and glasses were forced over her mouth and nose while she slept, interfering with her breathing. About forty days after the first disturbance, the spirit began to push needles into the left heel of the girl. These would simply appear out of nowhere—stuck in her bleeding flesh as she slept, even if she wore shoes and socks to bed. On one occasion fifty-five separate needles were removed from the foot of the howling girl.

In March 1966, spontaneous combustion occurred as Ferreira's clothing caught fire at school. Her bedroom burst into flames, severely burning Volpe as he tried to extinguish burning sheets, blankets, and pillows. Despite the bizarre and dangerous disturbances, Ferreira lived with Volpe for about a year, during which time the hauntings slowed, but never stopped.

Finally, Volpe took Ferreira to a medium who conducted a séance. While in a trance, the medium began to channel a character who spoke in a rough voice saying, "[Ferreira] was a witch. A lot of people suffered and I died because of her. Now we are making her suffer too."[70] Some believed these words and thought Ferreira was a reincarnation of a witch who lived in past years. Volpe recalled that talking poltergeists often lie, and so tried to cure the problems with nearly continuous prayer. While the most violent disturbances stopped, the girl continued to be the focus of thrown objects, especially fruit. Ferreira was very distraught from the endless attacks, and she finally committed suicide at the age of fourteen, drinking insecticide mixed into a soft drink. Despite the obvious appearance of suicide, some investigators debate whether Ferreira was killed by an outside force or not. As Brian A. Haughton writes on the "Maria José Ferreira—Poltergeist Victim" Web site:

> [Was] it a straightforward suicide? Did Maria take the poison deliberately, or did the poltergeist put it there. After all, it had materialized many other things in her presence. Another point is that it is very rare for a poltergeist to become so actively malicious. Usually poltergeist activity is characterized by the fact that, though it can cause serious trouble, usually no one is physically harmed. When a poltergeist case becomes violent, it is often termed an incidence of "demonic possession," as is suggested by the contempt by the spirits for exorcisms. Did the spirits believe that Maria had been a witch in a former life? It has to be remembered that spirits often lie, sometimes for no other reason than the sheer hell of it, and that the witch story may have been pure invention. [71]

Bribing an Evil Poltergeist

While Haughton's questions provide no answers, Playfair believes that Ferreira was possibly a victim of a black magic spell, a curse placed upon her by a magician who may have believed the girl was a witch. Such belief is common in Brazil and elsewhere in South America and Africa where people say that evil poltergeists can be hired by the living to torment enemies. The tortures are carried out through black magic—spells and rituals that can call up malevolent spirits. Brazilian psychic investigator Hernani Andrade explains:

> In every case of poltergeist activity . . . there has been evidence that somebody in the house could be the

Offerings to an Angry Spirit

Stories of homicidal poltergeists on murderous rampages have been told for thousands of years. One of the earliest tales, told by R.C. Finucane in *Appearances of the Dead: A Cultural History of Ghosts,* dates back to the second century A.D.:

It seems that when Ulysses was en route home from the Trojan [W]ar one of his sailors, Polites, raped a virgin and was stoned to death by the villagers. Ulysses sailed off without giving the body the benefit of a funeral. As a result the [poltergeist] of Polites began to attack and murder the local inhab-

itants. [An] oracle was consulted and . . . [she] declared that the villagers must build a temple-shrine to the [disembodied spirit] of Polites and every year offer him a virgin. This was done, and his [spirit] ceased to harass the general populace. One day the famous boxer Euthymos . . . arrived and fell in love with the virgin about to be offered. He waited for [Polites] to approach, then pounced. The boxer won the fight, driving the spirit into the sea forever. From that day forward the people suffered no more manifestations of Polites.

target of revenge. . . . It may be a former lover, . . . a jealous relation, a spiteful neighbor, or even a member of the same family bearing some trivial grudge. Any Brazilian is well aware that this country is full of backyard . . . black magic centers . . . where people use spirit forces for evil purposes.[72]

A black magician who wants to call up a poltergeist tries to strike a deal by bribing an evil apparition. Since the poltergeists allegedly want to enjoy the pleasures of life once again, they demand that the magician supply them with treats such as a meal, a cigar, a drink of rum, or even a sexual experience with a human victim. Playfair describes the relationship between the poltergeist and the black magician:

The spirit has the upper hand in all this. He calls the shots, he wants his meal left in a certain place at a certain time, and the rum and the cigar had better be of good quality. Incarnate man is ready to oblige, and it is remarkable how many members of Brazil's poorest classes, who are about as poor as anyone can be, will some-

how manage to lay out a magnificent banquet for a spirit who has agreed to work some magic for them when
they cannot afford to feed their own children properly.[73]

Believers in this form of black magic say that the evil poltergeists are inferior spirits who have not evolved to a high-
er consciousness after death. They are known as *exús*, spirits
who seem to have no morals at all. They will purportedly assault, torture, torment, and even kill their victims, as Playfair
writes: "Like Mafia gunmen, they do what the boss says without questions."[74]

Although *exús* are egotistical, unprincipled, and volatile,
they allegedly insist on observing formal rituals. Anyone who
accidentally disturbs the offerings of food, cigars, or liquor
made by a black magician might end up drawn into the evil
spell not intended for them. After this happens the victim's
life may become a living nightmare. This was the case for a
twenty-eight-year-old Brazilian woman known only as Marcia
F. In 1973, she was nearly destroyed because she purportedly interfered with forces of an evil poltergeist *exú* called up
through a black magic spell.

"Go On, Throw Yourself Out"

Marcia F. was on vacation near São Paulo, walking on a beach,
when she picked up a worn plaster statue, about six inches
high, that she found lying in the sand. Her aunt warned her
to leave it alone because it was a statue of the sea goddess
Yemanjé that someone had left on the beach as a religious offering. Marcia, who had a master's degree in psychology, dis-
missed her aunt's words as nonsense and took the fascinat-
ing statue home to her apartment.

Within days, Marcia was seemingly attacked by an unknown force. She became violently sick with food poisoning.
After she recovered from that, she inexplicably began to lose
weight and cough up blood as if she had tuberculosis, or TB.
As the illness continued, Marcia's skin turned greenish-yellow,

she began to lose her memory, and was unable to function at her job.

Marcia's health slowly returned, but she continued to feel under attack. While she was making dinner one night, a pressure cooker blew up in her face. She was showered with boiling beans and water and suffered second-degree burns on her hands, arms, face, and neck. At the same instant that this was happening, a photograph of Marcia allegedly jumped off the wall at her parent's apartment several miles away. Days later, Marcia's oven inexplicably exploded, blowing off the door and shooting out flames that nearly killed her. An engineer called in to investigate could find no mechanical causes for either of the kitchen disturbances.

After rationally examining her streak of bad luck Marcia came to believe that her illness and her kitchen accidents were simply coincidental. When a friend suggested that the statue

Pictured is a shrine to the Brazilian sea goddess Yemanjé. In 1973 a woman was reportedly tormented by an unknown force after she removed a statue of Yemanjé from a Brazilian beach.

of Yemanjé might be the problem, Marcia reacted, saying, "Nonsense. . . . How can a statue do anything? . . . There cannot be any relation between a statue and a burn or a dose of TB."[75]

Despite the words meant to reassure her friend—and herself—Marcia's problems soon escalated to suicidal depression. One afternoon a friend dropped her keys while crossing a busy street. When Marcia, who was behind her, bent over to pick up the keys, a light changed at a nearby intersection and cars raced forward, leaving the woman crouched between lanes. At that moment, Marcia felt like throwing herself under the wheels of a passing car and ending it all. The feeling passed and Marcia scrambled to safety, but a few days later, when she opened a window in her fifteenth-floor apartment, she had a compelling urge to jump to her death. She later recalled, "It was like a voice inside me saying 'go on, throw yourself out.'"[76] Over the course of the next several nights, Marcia sank deeper into depression as she felt sure that she was being sexually assaulted by a male poltergeist as she lay in bed.

Finally, Marcia visited a spiritualist who practiced the *Umbanda* religion based on ancient African belief in magic and spirits. At a friend's urging, Marcia took along the statue of Yemanjé. The spiritualist told her that her problems were the result of a black magic spell that had been cast upon her by an unknown person for removing the statue from the beach. When Marcia examined the statue, she believed the words of the spiritualist. All of the paint had been worn off except where Marcia had been hurt. There was paint in the exact places on the arms, neck, and face where she had been burned. A patch over the lung was where she might have had TB. Most ominously, the blue eyes remained painted, creating a fear in Marcia that she would soon be blinded. In desperation, Marcia accepted the unproved explanation of the spiritualist and returned the statue to where she had found it. Immediately thereafter the woman ceased to experience distressing events.

Skeptics say such onslaughts of physical and mental catastrophes are most likely a result of mental breakdowns.

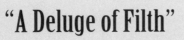

"A Deluge of Filth"

In rare cases where poltergeists attack, they have been known to target religious people. In the thirteenth century, Blessed Christina of Stommeln, an extremely devout woman, was allegedly assaulted by poltergeists that used violent, and often disgusting, tactics to drive her insane, as Alan Gauld and A.D. Cornell write in *Poltergeists*:

Christina was, apparently, subjected not just to the ordinary poltergeist annoyances—such as objects being moved and stones being thrown in her vicinity—but to many other even more unpleasant manifestations. Her bedclothes were pulled off and she herself was dragged about.

. . . Nails were thrust into her—sometimes they were found to be hot. . . . Hot stones were pressed into her body. Her clothes and shoes were cut to pieces. Her room, her clothes, sometimes her visitors were spattered with excrement. When an exorcism was attempted, a loud explosion was heard, and a deluge of filth descended on the exorcist. Christina suffered from numerous, and sometimes grotesque, hallucinations of a divine or diabolic character; and sometimes she was roughly dragged away to a distance as if by diabolic agency. All these phenomena ceased around the time at which she reached the menopause.

Perhaps Marcia had personal problems that were exacerbated by worry about having removed the statue, an act she subconsciously believed to have been terribly wrong. Such an explanation might account for her mental distress, but it does not address the explosions in the kitchen. Psychic investigator Andrade has his own answers:

You can use a knife to cut bread or to cut a man's throat, and so it is with the hidden powers of man; they can be turned to good or bad ends, though they remain the same powers. To produce a successful poltergeist, all you need is a group of bad spirits prepared to do your work for you, for a suitable reward, and a susceptible victim which is insufficiently developed spiritually to be able to resist.[77]

Deranged Mind or Demonic Spirit?

It is debatable whether Marcia's problems were caused by evil spirits or were instead strange manifestations of her own fears.

While the black magic concept is popular in some countries, modern psychic investigators remain convinced that poltergeist attacks are caused by the victims themselves. Gauld and Cornell offer a rather complicated theory of self-victimization based on human agents expressing extreme aggression toward themselves or others:

> Sometimes the phenomena have seemed undeniably . . . linked to the fears, frustrations and hostilities of a particular person. . . . Given these tendencies . . . one can readily imagine that the following state of affairs might arise: a poltergeist "agent" (often, though not always, a teenage girl), one whose phenomena have a violent or destructive tendency, has . . . attitudes of dislike and aggression towards a certain person—perhaps even, for complex psychological reasons, towards herself. Then the phenomena, reflecting these attitudes in ways which we don't understand, turn their violence more and more upon the disliked

Many modern researchers explain poltergeist activity, such as the seemingly inexplicable gashes on this woman's couch, as acts of self-victimization committed by troubled individuals.

person. Finally a . . . kind of paranoid state ensues in which the phenomena, really self-generated, are ascribed to some external persecutor [such as an evil poltergeist], and then assume a form which supports that belief. This state of affairs, unless interrupted in some way, becomes more or less self-perpetuating. [78]

Such complex explanations have more to do with psychology than the supernatural and offer little comfort to victims. Nonetheless, theories are all that people have to explain the bizarre phenomena that can ruin lives and drive victims mad. This dark side of the human experience may be traced to a deranged mind or a demonic spirit. Perhaps both are at work when poltergeists attack, wound, and kill.

Notes

Introduction: Noisy Spirits

1. Alan Gauld and A.D. Cornell, *Poltergeists*, London: Routledge & Kegan Paul, 1979, p. 4.

Chapter 1: Poltergeist Phenomena

2. Herbert Thurston, *Ghosts and Poltergeists*, Chicago: Henry Regnery, 1954, p. 2.
3. A.R.G. Owen, *Can We Explain the Poltergeist?*, New York: Helix, 1964, p. 2.
4. Owen, *Can We Explain the Poltergeist?*, p. 2.
5. Gauld and Cornell, *Poltergeists*, p. 67.
6. Quoted in Owen, *Can We Explain the Poltergeist?*, p. 96.
7. Quoted in Thurston, *Ghosts and Poltergeists*, p. 342.
8. Thurston, *Ghosts and Poltergeists*, p. 342.
9. Quoted in William G. Roll, *The Poltergeist*, Garden City, NY: Nelson Doubleday, 1972, p. 23.
10. Roll, *The Poltergeist*, pp. 18–19.
11. Quoted in James Houran and Rense Lange, eds., *Hauntings and Poltergeists*, Jefferson, NC: McFarland, 2001, p. 130.
12. D. Scott Rogo, *On the Track of the Poltergeist*, Englewood Cliffs, NJ: Prentice-Hall, 1986, p. 47.
13. Rogo, *On the Track of the Poltergeist*, p. 54.
14. Owen, *Can We Explain the Poltergeist?*, p. 179.
15. Quoted in Owen, *Can We Explain the Poltergeist?*, p. 182.
16. Quoted in D. Scott Rogo, *Minds and Motion: The Riddle of Psychokinesis*, New York: Taplinger, 1978, pp. 53–54.
17. Owen, *Can We Explain the Poltergeist?*, pp. 11–12.

Chapter 2: Poltergeists, Possession, and Exorcism

18. Raymond Bayless, *The Enigma of the Poltergeist*, West Nyack, NY: Parker, 1967, p. 160.
19. Quoted in Bayless, *The Enigma of the Poltergeist*, p. 166.
20. Quoted in George Lincoln Burr, ed., *Narratives of the Witchcraft Cases 1648–1706*, New York: Barnes & Noble, 1975, p. 159.
21. Bayless, *The Enigma of the Poltergeist*, p. 168.
22. Quoted in Colin Wilson, *Poltergeist!: A Study in Destructive Haunting*, St. Paul, MN: Llewellyn, 1993, p. 44.
23. Quoted in Wilson, *Poltergeist!*, p. 45.
24. Quoted in Wilson, *Poltergeist!*, p. 45.
25. Quoted in Thurston, *Ghosts and Poltergeists*, p. 111.
26. Quoted in Thurston, *Ghosts and Poltergeists*, pp. 112–13.
27. Quoted in Thurston, *Ghosts and Poltergeists*, p. 118.
28. Quoted in Thurston, *Ghosts and Poltergeists*, p. 121.

29. Quoted in Thurston, *Ghosts and Poltergeists*, p. 125.

30. Quoted in Gauld and Cornell, *Poltergeists*, p. 159.

31. Quoted in D. Scott Rogo, *The Poltergeist Experience: Investigations into Ghostly Phenomena*, New York: Penguin, 1979, p. 191.

32. Quoted in Rogo, *The Poltergeist Experience*, p. 192.

33. Rogo, *The Poltergeist Experience*, p. 194.

34. Guy Playfair, *This House Is Haunted*, New York: Stein and Day, 1980, p. 290.

35. Gauld and Cornell, *Poltergeists*, pp. 158–59.

Chapter 3: Hunting Poltergeists

36. Katherine Ramsland, *Ghost: Investigating the Other Side*, New York: Thomas Dunne, 2001, p. 12.

37. Harry Price, *The Most Haunted House in England*, London: Longmans, Green, 1990, p. 111.

38. Quoted in Price, *The Most Haunted House in England*, pp. 214–15.

39. Price, *The Most Haunted House in England*, p. 5.

40. Peter Underwood, *Ghosts and How to See Them*, London: Anaya, 1993, p. 114.

41. Quoted in Underwood, *Ghosts and How to See Them*, p. 102.

42. Roll, *The Poltergeist*, p. 201.

43. Underwood, *Ghosts and How to See Them*, p. 106.

44. Underwood, *Ghosts and How to See Them*, p. 102.

45. Roll, *The Poltergeist*, p. 205.

46. Hans Holzer, *Ghost Hunter*, Indianapolis: Bobbs-Merrill, 1963, p. 17.

47. Playfair, *This House Is Haunted*, p. 48.

48. Underwood, *Ghosts and How to See Them*, p. 105.

49. Underwood, *Ghosts and How to See Them*, p. 112.

50. Underwood, *Ghosts and How to See Them*, p. 106.

51. Quoted in Roll, *The Poltergeist*, p. xi.

Chapter 4: Poltergeist Communications

52. Bayless, *The Enigma of the Poltergeist*, p. 79.

53. Wilson, *Poltergeist!*, pp. 110–11.

54. Quoted in Thurston, *Ghosts and Poltergeists*, p. 13.

55. Owen, *Can We Explain the Poltergeist?*, p. 239.

56. Quoted in Wilson, *Poltergeist!*, p. 111.

57. Quoted in Wilson, *Poltergeist!*, p. 114.

58. Quoted in Wilson, *Poltergeist!*, p. 116.

59. Troy Taylor, "Borley Rectory: The History of 'The Most Haunted House in England,'" 2000. http://www.prairie ghosts.com/brectory.html.

60. Quoted in Price, *The Most Haunted House in England*, p. 159.

61. Quoted in Price, *The Most Haunted House in England*, p. 164.

62. Quoted in Owen, *Can We Explain the Poltergeist?*, p. 240.

63. Bayless, *The Enigma of the Poltergeist*, pp. 79-80.

Chapter 5: When Poltergeists Attack

64. Gauld and Cornell, *Poltergeists*, p. 116.

65. Quoted in Thurston, *Ghosts and Poltergeists*, p. 38.

66. Quoted in Rogo, *The Poltergeist Experience*, p. 183.
67. Quoted in Roll, *The Poltergeist*, p. 56.
68. Roll, *The Poltergeist*, p. 68.
69. Guy Playfair, *The Indefinite Boundary*, New York: St. Martin's, 1976, p. 242.
70. Quoted in Playfair, *The Indefinite Boundary*, p. 246.
71. Brian A. Haughton, "Maria José Ferreira—Poltergeist Victim," Mysterious People, 2002. http://www.mysterious people.com/Maria_Ferreira.htm.
72. Quoted in Wilson, *Poltergeist!*, pp. 236–37.
73. Playfair, *The Indefinite Boundary*, pp. 253–54.
74. Playfair, *The Indefinite Boundary*, p. 254.
75. Quoted in Playfair, *The Indefinite Boundary*, pp. 249–50.
76. Quoted in Playfair, *The Indefinite Boundary*, p. 250.
77. Quoted in Wilson, *Poltergeist!*, p. 237.
78. Gauld and Cornell, *Poltergeists*, pp. 116–17.

For Further Reading

Books

Terry O'Neill, ed. *Ghosts and Poltergeists*. San Diego: Greenhaven, 2003. Articles debating the reality of the mysterious phenomena allegedly caused by supernatural spirits.

Peter Underwood, *Ghosts and How to See Them*. London: Anaya, 1993. A book that details methods for finding ghosts, photographing them, and communicating with them, written by a psychic researcher who is president of the Ghost Club, founded in the United Kingdom in 1862.

Graham Watkins, *Ghosts and Poltergeists*. New York: Rosen Publishing Group, 2002. Discusses some real-life cases of ghosts and hauntings, as well as some of the theories about them.

Colin Wilson, *Ghosts and the Supernatural*. New York: DK, 1998. Relates purportedly true accounts of ghosts, poltergeists, phantom animals, and other supernatural wonders and discusses research on such phenomena.

Internet Sources

Committee for the Scientific Investigation of Claims of the Paranormal, *CSIOP Online*, www.csicop.org. This site undertakes critical investigation of paranormal claims and examines them from a scientific viewpoint.

The Ghost Club, "Ghost Club Talk: John Spencer On Poltergeists," www.ghostclub.org.uk/. This is a site hosted by the Ghost Club, founded in England in 1862. The club is concerned with ghosts, hauntings, and other paranormal activities. The "Investigations" section is particularly interesting, with ghost hunts, poltergeist sightings, and photographs.

Ghosts of the Prairie, "Borley Rectory: The History of 'The Most Haunted House in England,'" www.prairieghosts.com/brectory.html. An in-depth examination into the apparitions of Borley Rectory and the ghost hunters who tried to find them.

Works Consulted

Books

Raymond Bayless, *The Enigma of the Poltergeist.* West Nyack, NY: Parker, 1967. An investigation into poltergeist activity and the association of poltergeists with ghosts and witchcraft throughout the ages.

George Lincoln Burr, ed., *Narratives of the Witchcraft Cases 1648–1706.* New York: Barnes & Noble, 1975. This book, first published in 1914, contains some of the original court transcripts of the Salem witch trials along with letters and essays written by Cotton and Increase Mather and others.

Richard Cavendish, *The Encyclopedia of the Unexplained: Magic, Occultism, and Parapsychology.* New York: McGraw-Hill, 1974. A comprehensive listing of paranormal phenomena that offers explanations from psychic researchers as to the causes of these mysterious activities.

Catherine Crowe, *The Night-Side of Nature.* Wellingborough, England: Aquarian, 1986. A classic work of research into ghostly phenomena from the Victorian era, first published in 1848.

R.C. Finucane, *Appearances of the Dead: A Cultural History of Ghosts.* London: Junction, 1982. Ghosts throughout history from classical Greece through the Middle Ages and into the twentieth century.

Alan Gauld and A.D. Cornell, *Poltergeists.* London: Routledge & Kegan Paul, 1979. The first part of this book contains descriptions of dozens of poltergeist cases throughout history while the second part consists of the conclusions of the authors who investigated and analyzed the cases.

Hans Holzer, *Ghost Hunter.* Indianapolis: Bobbs-Merrill, 1963. The exploits of a widely published psychic investigator in and around New York City as he contacts ghosts in fashionable apartments and eighteenth-century farmhouses.

James Houran and Rense Lange, eds., *Hauntings and Poltergeists.* Jefferson, NC: McFarland, 2001. A study, written by the world's leading authorities, of the cultural, physical, and psychological aspects of ghosts.

A.R.G. Owen, *Can We Explain the Poltergeist?* New York: Helix, 1964. A scientific explanation of poltergeists, with chapters about real, fake, and unexplainable manifestations.

Guy Playfair, *The Indefinite Boundary.* New York: St. Martin's, 1976. An investigation into the relationships between atoms, matter, and other scientific theories, and those of supernatural phenomena such as PK energy, telepathy, and other psychic forces.

Guy Playfair, *This House Is Haunted.* New York: Stein and Day, 1980. The case of Janet Harper, an eleven-year-old girl in Enfield, England, who was the epicenter of extreme poltergeist activity allegedly witnessed by the author.

Harry Price, *The Most Haunted House in England.* London: Longmans, Green, 1990. Originally published in 1940 and written by the world's first ghost hunter, this book tells the story of the ten-year investigation into the noisy and persistent ghosts of Borley Rectory in Essex.

Katherine Ramsland, *Ghost: Investigating the Other Side.* New York: Thomas Dunne, 2001. The adventures of a forensic and clinical psychologist as she becomes a world-class ghost hunter.

D. Scott Rogo, *Minds and Motion: The Riddle of Psychokinesis.* New York: Taplinger, 1978. An examination of PK energy said to be responsible for poltergeist incidents and other unexplainable events from spoon bending to psychic healing.

———, *On the Track of the Poltergeist.* Englewood Cliffs, NJ: Prentice-Hall, 1986. According to the author, this book contains the true stories of his investigations into poltergeist activity.

———, *The Poltergeist Experience: Investigations into Ghostly Phenomena.* New York: Penguin, 1979. In this volume, the author blames poltergeist activity on the victims, concluding that they subconsciously manifest these events as a consequence of deep psychological conflicts, repressed hatred, and buried frustrations.

William G. Roll, *The Poltergeist.* Garden City, NY: Nelson Doubleday, 1972. A study of several poltergeist cases by a world-famous authority on the phenomenon who is one of the founders of the Psychical Research Foundation, which investigates reports of poltergeists.

Sacheverell Sitwell, *Poltergeists.* New York: University, 1959. Ten source descriptions of poltergeist cases from the past four centuries, reprinted from original texts, with comments by the author.

Herbert Thurston, *Ghosts and Poltergeists.* Chicago: Henry Regnery, 1954. A book by a noted historian and scholar who hunts for a natural explanation for the recorded activities of poltergeists and ghosts.

Colin Wilson, *Poltergeist!: A Study in Destructive Haunting.* St. Paul, MN: Llewellyn, 1993. Examples of hostile ghosts and negative psychic phenomena as a result of black magic, psychokinesis, fairies, and other causes.

Internet Sources

Robert Todd Carroll, "The Ideomotor Effect," The Skeptic's Dictionary, 2002. http://skepdic.com/ideomotor.html.

Richard Chamberlain, "Lithobolia: or, the Stone-Throwing Devil," Salem State

College, (no date). www.salem.mass.edu/ ~ebaker/chadweb/lithoweb.htm.

Brian A. Haughton, "Maria José Ferreira— Poltergeist Victim," Mysterious People, 2002. http://www.mysteriouspeople.com/ Maria_Ferreira.htm.

Joe Nickell, "Exorcism! Driving Out the Nonsense," CSICOP, January/February 2001. www.csicop.org/si/2001-01/i-files.html.

Uktouristinfo.com, "The Gazetteer of Mysterious Britain," 2002. www.uktourist info.com/myst/gazetteer/gazlondon32.htm.

Index

Picture Credits

Cover photo: PBNJ Productions/CORBIS
© Bettmann/CORBIS, 34, 35, 65, 78
Dr. Susan Blackmore/Fortean Picture Library, 85
Fortean Picture Library, 16, 71, 74, 75
Getty Images, 40
Dr. Elmar R. Gruber/Fortean Picture Library, 53
Adam Hart-Davis/Fortean Picture Library, 30, 87
© Dave G. Houser/CORBIS, 92
© Hulton-Deutsch Collection/CORBIS, 51
Mary Evans Picture Library, 11, 37, 42, 62, 68, 82
Guy Lyon Playfair/Fortean Picture Library, 26, 47, 58, 95
Time Life Pictures/Getty Images, 15, 19, 22, 25, 57
Ken Webster/Fortean Picture Library, 12, 43

About the Author

Stuart A. Kallen is the author of more than 180 nonfiction books for children and young adults. He has written on topics ranging from the theory of relativity to the history of rock and roll. In addition, Mr. Kallen has written award-winning children's videos and television scripts. In his spare time, he is a singer/songwriter/guitarist in San Diego, California.